SAUCE

BY
RONNIE BARKER

CORONET BOOKS
HODDER AND STOUGHTON

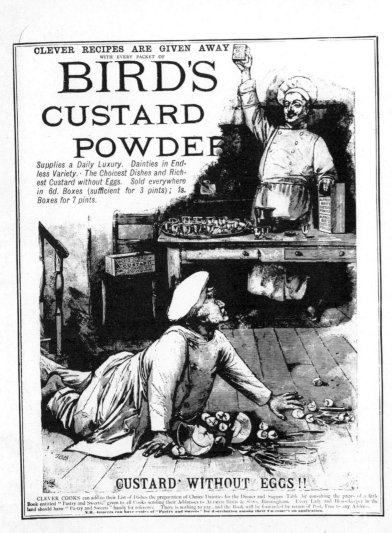

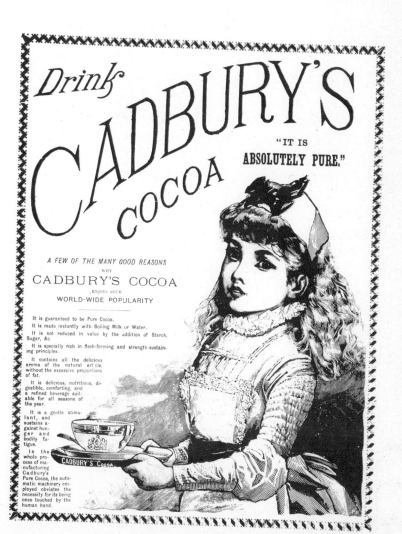

Acknowledgements

I would like to acknowledge the help and advice of Brian Long; and also the generosity of Gladys, Duchess of Bloemfontein, who, during the preparation of this book, accommodated me for a whole week without letting me spend a penny.

R. B.

CREDITS

Cartoons from *Punch* are reproduced by permission of the Proprietors of *Punch*; the illustrations by Donald McGill on pages 98–99 are reproduced by permission of Basil N. Buckland. Ronnie Barker also acknowledges his debt to the wonderful artists of *La Vie Parisienne*. It has been found impossible to trace the holders of the copyright to certain illustrations. We apologise for credits thus omitted, and if informed of the fact, will gladly rectify the matter in future editions.

Instructions for the Moving Pictures

Hold the pages of the book between the thumb and forefinger of the right hand, and, starting at this page, flick through, and you will UNDOUBTEDLY SEE WHAT THE BUTLER SAW.

Flicking it in reverse will, of course, cause the young lady to get dressed remarkably quickly and walk out backwards.

Please yourself.

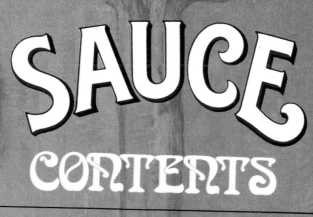

SAUCE

CONTENTS

CORONET BOOKS
HODDER AND STOUGHTON

(New readers start anywhere)

THE GENIE IN THE BOTTLE

THIS BOOK is meant to delight the eye. It is intended, as most culinary sauces do, to tickle the palate. The dictionary describes "sauce" as "a thing mixed"—a tinge, a tincture, a touch, a dash, a sprinkling, a seasoning, a soupçon, a smack; and within these pages I have tried to provide all of these by word and picture. But mostly, you will find, by picture.

It is a scrapbook of popular postcard and magazine art of days gone by, and so many of the pictures require no explanation—all they need is to be looked at. I do hope you find most of them well worth it.

The other meaning of the word "sauce", apart from its condiment sense, is, of course, impudence; and the pictures are undeniably cheeky, the rhymes robust, racy, and even raucous in places. The girls are either pert, pretty, and piquante (a word very much a favourite of the sauce manufacturers) or they are meaty, monstrous, or merciless, as in some of the more heavy-handed postcards.

The Genie in the Bottle continued

The main period from which these weird and wonderful creatures emerge is the first twenty years of the century. A few are later—one or two earlier; but for the most part they are the product of the Music-Hall years, when sixpence would buy you a passport into the gaudy, exciting world of the red-nosed comic, the terrifying trapeze acts, the ample-bosomed singer of popular songs, and those gorgeous, painted girls of the chorus, who danced as one, seeming to have no individual personality of their own at all; until suddenly, in the middle of the third number, you noticed the little dark one second from the end, and thereafter concentrated on her particular skills throughout the rest of the programme.

The jokes were rough and ready, and many of them would be so dated as to mean nothing to an audience today. However, some still have a timeless humour about them, and these are the ones I have included in the following pages. You will find one or two music-hall songs scattered about, illustrated by postcards of the time—and although a song isn't much without its music, there may be enough pungency left to enable you to get a whiff of the gas-lit, cigar-smoke-filled atmosphere of that glittering fun-palace that is no more.

However, my main aim was to fill the book as full as I could with colour, glamour and comedy—and I have managed to cram in 770 illustrations into 124 pages. I hope they speak for themselves, with few further interruptions from me; and that there is something to laugh at on every one.

Ronnie Barker

MOULIN ROUGE
Grand Chahut -- The French Cancan

DADDIES SAUCE

I'm coming home by rail.

MY OWN Daddie was born in 1906, which means that he was a toddler when the picture-postcard craze was at its height, and he grew up through that long, long war, emerging into manhood just as the twenties got really roaring.

So Daddies sauce was definitely that of the twenties—a time when the world was accelerating by the minute, and even the fastest of girls had to move a bit to keep up with it. The next few pages are devoted, in most cases, to the girls who managed it.

There's a girl wanted here!

A FAIR MYSTERY.

A Fine Pear from

PULBOROUGH.

This just shows you what a lady is on the Rolling Staircase.

DADDIES SAUCE

Maid: The Missus says there's been a great deal of water in the milk lately.

Milkman: Well, you can't blame the cows, can 'ee? This be thirsty weather, poor things!

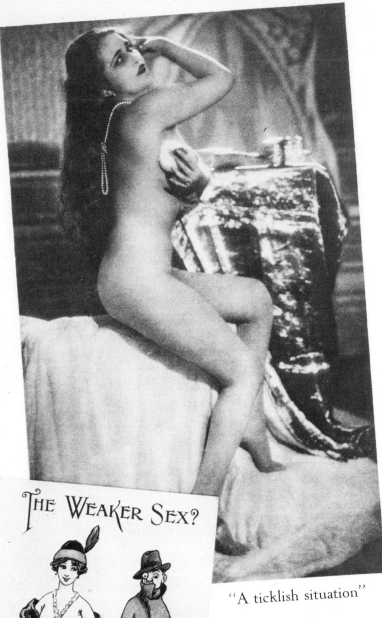

"A ticklish situation"

THE WEAKER SEX?

"Did you ring Sir"

"TWO PENNYWORTH OF DOG BISCUITS, PLEASE."
"YES SIR, SHALL I WRAP THEM IN PAPER, OR WILL YOU EAT THEM HERE?"

A POOR SHIPWRECKED GIRL ON A RAFT
WAS HAILED BY A PASSING CRAFT.
"WHAT'S THE THING SIGNIFY
THAT YOU'VE HOISTED ON HIGH?"
SAID SHE, "THAT I SIT IN A DRAFT."

THERE WAS A YOUNG BANDSMEN OF DEE,
TRIED TO PLAY WITH A GIRL ON HIS KNEE,
BUT THE POINT OF THE JOKE IS HE
STRUCK THE WRONG NOTE
AND THE WEDDING'S ON THURSDAY AT 3.

THERE WAS A YOUNG GIRL NAMED BIANCA
WHO SLEPT WHILE THE SHIP LAY AT ANCHOR
SHE AWOKE IN DISMAY
WHEN SHE HEARD THE MATE SAY
"NOW LIFT UP THE TOP-SHEET AND SPANKER"

THE
HAREM
LILY
UP-TO-DATE.

HAVE YOU ANYTHING IN THE SHAPE
OF A CUCUMBER?
YES MISS, A BANANA. HOW WILL
THAT SUIT?

TAKE A FRIENDS
ADVICE AND DON'T WEAR
MUSLIN FROCKS!

A little fresh 'air from
EASTBOURNE.

A rather sad occurrence
Can here be clearly seen
I once used fertiliser
Instead of Brilliantine.
It's really most embarrassing—
Now it has come to pass
That every time I raise my hat
I show the girls my grass.

VELY LOAD, JUST ARRIVED
BLACKPOOL.

DADDIES SAUCE

MANY MERRY XMAS DAYS AND MAY YOU KEEP 'EM UP LIVELY

Let your Spirits HOLD UP
and you'll certainly find
They'll keep you to-day
in HIGH feather.
And I shall be pleased.
if Dame Fortune so kind
Let's SUS·PEND·ER
few moments
together.

Three cheers for the stocking!
One glimpse (oh, how shocking)
Of leg wrapped in sensual silk
Causes scandals, sensations,
The downfall of nations,
And men to come home with the milk.

The GLAD EYE.

PUT ME AMONGST THE GIRLS

WILL YOU PLAY WITH ME TO-NIGHT

WHAT'S YOUR LITTLE GAME?

"I THINK WE'VE MET BEFORE"

"I think we've met before
   Was it at the clothing store?"
Said the trousers, with a grin.
"Yes, I'm sure it must have been,"
"No," replied the underwear,
"It was on a bedroom chair.
And she's hoping he'll forget her—
P'raps the less that's said, the better!"

NOW YOU'RE MARRIED
I WISH YOU JOY!

DADDIES SAUCE

Old Lady: Five shillings worth of three
  halfpenny stamps, please. How much is that?
New Girl: Er—That will be seven and sixpence.

"'Alf a pint, miss, please."
"No, you're too late. The clock's struck."
"Go on—it ain't finished humming yet."

"A two-penny mousetrap
please, as quick as possible.
Mother wants to catch a train."

"I've hurt my hand in the
hot water, cook!"
"Ah, sure, it serves you
right. You should have
felt the water before you
put your hand in."

Queen of the Chorus: Our
  leading lady couldn't
    appear tonight.
Maid: Why not, miss?
Q of the C: A moth got
  into her dressing room
  and ate both her
  costumes.

Barber: We was discussing National Service, wasn't we,
  last time I shaved you? Have you joined up yet?
Customer: I don't know, I haven't taken the plaster off yet.

THE HAREM SKIRT HAS STOPPED ALL THIS SORT OF THING.

DADDIES SAUCE

Priscilla Jones had great big
   knees
Yet never ceased to show 'em—
Like champagne bottles stood
   on end
Each one a Jeroboam.

Although her friends all called
   her plump
She thought her shape
   perfection;
She crossed her legs at the
   flower show
And won the Marrow section.

I AM GETTING A MOUTHFUL
OF FRESH 'AIR

WHAT KIND OF A-TACK

She: Only last night you called me the
apple of your eye.
He: Well, what of it?
She: What's the matter—gorn orf fruit,
'or something?

DADDIES SAUCE

A GOOD DEED.

CUSTOMER (who has inquired the price of every article on the counter) : "And this pest exterminator– how is it applied ?"
WEARY CHEMIST (emphatically) : "You take a tablespoonful every half-hour, madam."

"Oh, shocking !!"

Bloke come in the shop today and says,
"I can't see you properly. You're all fuzzy.
Do I need stronger glasses?"
and I says, "No, fewer."

LAST SUMMER MARY WAS IN THE SWING, AND HER YOUNG MAN **PUSHED** HER.

THIS SUMMER MARY IS DOING THE PUSHING!

Doctor: When I feel run down, I take my wife away for the week end. That's what you should do.

Patient: Very well Doctor, when will it suit your wife?

OUR DOCTOR

SEEING A LADY PATIENT

He: No can come with you. Me gottee see dentist.

She: Nonsense—I'll soon cure that round at my flat. Two thirty all right?

He: Tooth hurtee all right, that's why me gottee see dentist.

LEAP YEAR

Marry me and I'll lay you 10 to 1.

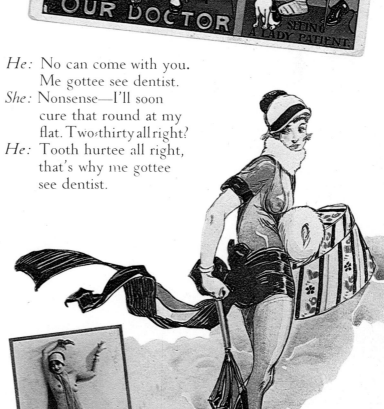

"The Family Features"

Drawn by *Leonard Smith.*

"Smithers. I am surprised to see you about here still! Why are you not at the Front?"
"Cos there ain't no milk at that end, mum!"

BUT HE CAN'T.

"So that is the man you want to marry.
What does he mean when he says he's a wood-worker?"
"I think. Daddy, he means he would if he could."

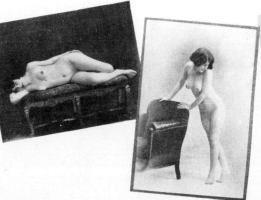

DADDiES
SAUCE

I'm not so good as I ought to be,
  As Mother said to Dad;
But one thing I'm perfectly certain of,
On the whole I'm
  not so bad.

I WOULD'NT MIND GETTING INTO HOT WATER WITH YOU.

A FORTNIGHT HERE WOULD MAKE YOUR CHEEKS QUITE ROSY.

WET PAINT

This snap of Auntie
Maud reveals
The influence
of liquor—
She'd had too many
sherries, and
Was trying to tempt
the vicar.

I am holding my own—

ACCIDENTS WILL HAPPEN AT HOME AS WELL AS AT THE FRONT.

NEW STYLES

THE LATEST FASHIONS IN FIG-LEAVES

WANT A NEW SUIT SIR? OUR LADY ASSISTANT WILL MEASURE YOU!

THE LAUNDRY MAID.

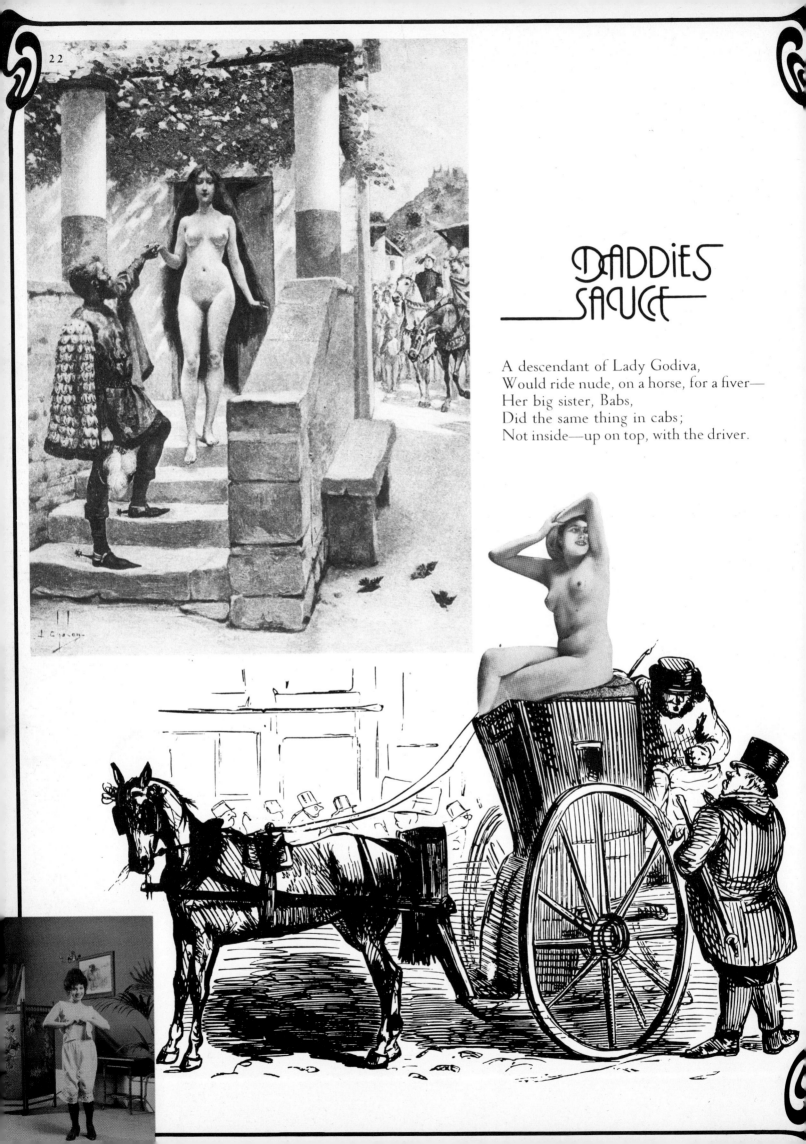

DADDIES SAUCE

A descendant of Lady Godiva,
Would ride nude, on a horse, for a fiver—
Her big sister, Babs,
Did the same thing in cabs;
Not inside—up on top, with the driver.

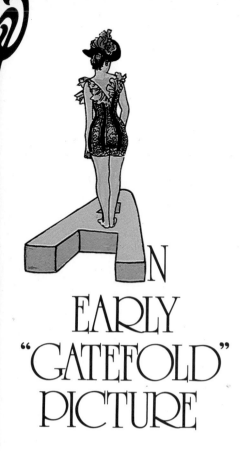

AN EARLY "GATEFOLD" PICTURE

This photograph, in an early Art magazine, was printed at twice this size, and was described in the pages of the magazine as being "an example of a classic pose, for serious students of sculpture"

This didn't prevent it being framed and hung in many clubs and saloons, in the United States as well as in Britain, for the even more serious students of snooker and shove-hapenny.

The reason for the colour is presumably artistic, and the fact that the model's name was actually Miss Greenbaum must have been merely a happy coincidence.

AT THE SEASIDE IT'S QUITE THE THING
TO BE PHOTOGRAPHED SEATED ON A DONKEY.

SOCIETY GOSSIP

LORD HOTSTUFF SPENT A LONG
TIME AT THE DRESS EXHIBITION THIS MORNING !

The Double Meaning

Here, and on the next couple of pages, a few examples of the basis of most jokes—the double meaning.

The marvellous thing about a joke with a double meaning is that it can only mean one thing . .

YOU CAN SEE BY THE LINE I AM
SENDING THAT I HAVE
NOT MUCH ON AT PRESENT

PLEASE MA'AM, HERE'S THE RAILWAY PORTER
COME TO TAKE YOUR BAGS OFF.

I CANNOT BEAR THIS PLACE ANY LONGER.

EVERY SEAT FULL!

(DANCING MASTER) "HIGHER MISS HIGHER"
(DANCER) "WHAT, FOR FIFTEEN BOB A WEEK."

DO YOU WANT A BED-WARMER SIR?

"I felt an awful ass."

THE MODERN GIRL IS SIMPLY RIPPING!

A nice bit of mutton for the week-end, Mister P

You don't kiss me as often now as you used to when I was younger dear.
Ah, darling, a great deal has come between us since then.

THE BARE IDEA!

CAN YOU SEE MY BAGS PORTER?
NO MISS; NOT QUITE.

"HENRY, IT'S TWENTY TO ONE!"
"ALL RI', I'LL HAVE FIVE BOB EACH WAY!"

DADDIES SAUCE

"Quick George, my cheeks will get sunburned!" get the cold cream.

COMING DOWN

SALE

A VARIETY OF ARTICLES WILL BE ON SHOW

YOUR INSPECTION INVITED

DASHES & HOSIERY

EVERY PICTURE TELLS A STORY!

I suppose I should earn enough to live on between the two.

YOUNG LADY WANTED To Exhibit Our NEW PINK & WHITE STOCKINGS AND SELF LOCKING SUSPENDERS APPLY AT FRILLS & Co HIGH STREET

"It's a bad job about Mrs. Jones' husband. He's had to have his tonsils cut out."
"Law, and she is so fond of children, too!"

REMARKABLY TIGHT AT THE BOTTOM.

"DON'T LET IT GO ANY FARTHER."

"I WANT A BLOUSE, Please"
"Yes Miss, WHAT BUST?"
"I DON'T KNOW, I DIDN'T HEAR ANYTHING!"

"I GET TEN SHILLINGS A WEEK AND PARTIAL BOARD"
"IS THAT ALL? WHY I GET THIRTY AND MY WHOLE BOARD!"

THE BEAUTIFUL LA SMILO! IN THE GREAT CLASSICAL TABLEAUX VENUS, THE ARTIST'S MODEL ETC.,

LAST NIGHTS NIGHTLY AT 6.20 AND TICKET OFFICE

I'M GOING TO "SEE" WITH A SAILOR!

GRAND-DADDIES SAUCE

LET US, having taken a gander at what might be described as sauce for the goose in my daddie's day now progress backwards, if that is possible. (It *is* actually possible—ask the cox of an Oxford eight.) We now look back on the good old days of Grandaddie; those times described as the naughty nineties, the turn of the century, the halcyon days of an Empire on which the sun never set, the age of elegance; the time when, as my own particular Grandfather used to say, "You could buy three pennyworth of chips and still have change from sixpence."

The jokes (and the girls) of his day were rather more covered up; the jokes more longwinded and physical, the girls more stout-limbed and winsome.

Nevertheless, the naughtiness of the nineties can be easily detected in the following pages—be it the girl in the toilet with her umbrella up, the can-can dancer with her leg up, or the fishing-boat with its bottom up.

GRAND-DADDIES SAUCE

"And how old are *you*, my dear?"
"Twelve, sir."
"Twelve? Good gracious! By the time I was your age I was seventeen!"

"There she is. George wants us to turn her upside down and tar her bottom." (Maiden lady leaves in a hurry.)

THE MAN WITH ONE HAIR.

He was not bald, for, on his shining cranium
Remained one hair, its colour pink geranium.
Oh! how he idolised that single hair
That, last of loved ones, grew luxuriant there.

* *

He counted it each morning, fondly viewed it
This way and that way ; carefully shampooed it ;
Combed it and brushed it, scented it and oiled it,
Dared scarce to put his hat on, lest he spoiled it.

* *

In evening dress, arrayed for swell society,
He'd part it in the middle for variety.
Often he'd curl it, train it on his brow
In navy fashion, as our middies now.

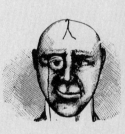

* *

Omitting nothing, with devoted care
He'd pet his hirsute pride, his single hair !
But, sad to say (ah ! heavy was the blow !)
There came a day, a day of direst woe.

* *

'Twas in his soup it fell ; he quick espied it ;
He rescued it, and on his napkin dried it :
His only hair, his pet, his flowing tress.
Chill was his forehead, deep his heart's distress.

* *

"I'm bald at last !" he cried in bitter grief ;
"My only hair has fallen like a leaf !
What! ho! A taxidermist !" shouted he ;
"I'll have it stuffed, for all the world to see !"

(*And so he did.*)

"Roses are Red
Violets are Blue
Mabel wears white ones
and I do, too."

Gruss aus MARIENBAD.

NOTES FROM MY DIARY

Dear Diary,

Yesterday, the whole academy went on a ramble down to the coast near Aix-les-Bains. It was Mrs. Todhunter's idea that, as it was a Nature Ramble, we should all get back to Nature by not wearing anything. You should have seen her! Unfortunately, you can't because she was taking the photographs. The sea was a bit rough, as you notice, but there was certainly plenty to be seen on the sea-shore that day. We had a splendid time, and lots of us caught things—crabs, colds, etcetera. Later we moved inland a little, and examined the delights of field, woodland, and hedgerow.

Here are some of the things we saw on our journey.

Notes from my diary (continued)

The ground was a bit rough, and people kept falling over, as you can see—but it was all grand fun. We found an enormous cobweb among the ferns, which looked as if it had been spun by an elephant. I must say I thought some of the girls were awfully brave to sit in the bracken with that sort of creature about. Altogether a very jolly day. Home to tea, and bed by nine-thirty, as usual.

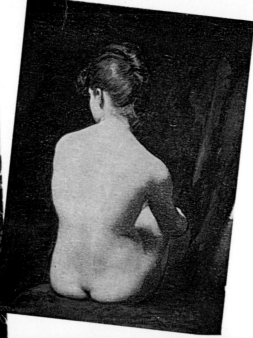

He: There's many a good tune played on an old viol.
She: And there's quite a few vile ones played as well.

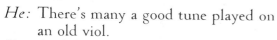

Old Jack, who's ninety-one, proposed to strapping Elsie Wills.
He went round to his doctors' for a check-up, and some pills.
"This marriage could prove fatal," said his doctor in surprise.
To which old Jack replied, "So what? If she dies, she dies!"

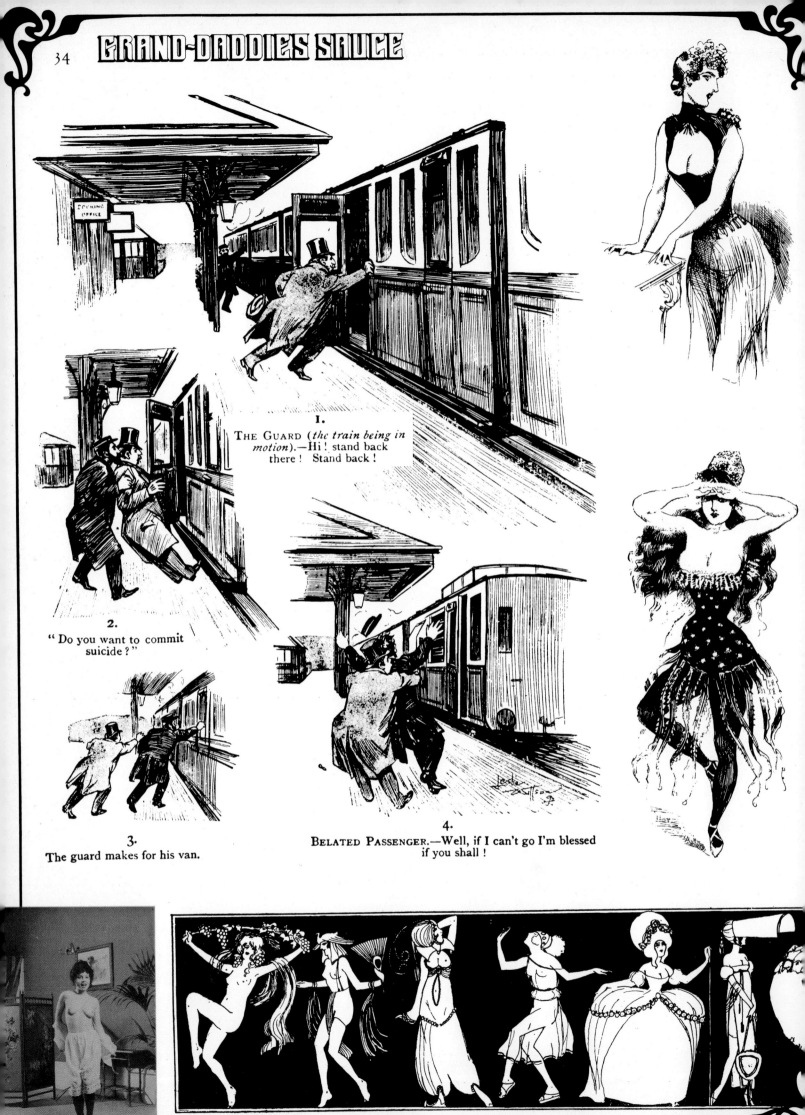

I.
THE GUARD (*the train being in motion*).—Hi! stand back there! Stand back!

2.
"Do you want to commit suicide?"

3.
The guard makes for his van.

4.
BELATED PASSENGER.—Well, if I can't go I'm blessed if you shall!

GODDESS OF PEACE

Nur einen Anlauf braucht's

Soll ich's riskiren!?

Courage!

Jetzt gieb's kein Zurück mehr

geschehen ist's!

A girl (who was normally bright)
Tried some stunts on her cycle one night;
She went off the rails
When the wind took her sails—
Her demise can be seen on the right.

BUT THERE'S ALWAYS ROOM FOR A GIRL

LOVE ONE ANOTHER

GALLERY 3/

DOUBLE BED 15/-

2/6

I'm as snug as a bug in a rug

KEEP SMILING, DEAREST.

WHAT SHALL I WEAR?
(some suggestions)

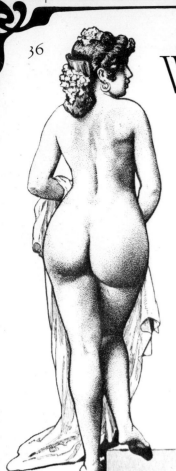

A sparkling wine—now there's
a dress
That might appeal to you.
But take care—if your label
shows
Your vintage is on view.

Dressed as a bundle of cigars
Is dangerous, she's found;
Last night, among the gentlemen
She twice got handed round.

"The Net Result"

This military maiden is
Already fast retreating
For fear the enemy approach
And give her drum a beating.

GRAND-DADDIES SAUCE

"Fashion on the Brain"   "Corn on the Nob"

La chasse aux Mouettes!!

Henne und Küchlein!
Le bain de la poule et ses poussins!

L'Etoile

Seestern

Der Kuss der Welle.

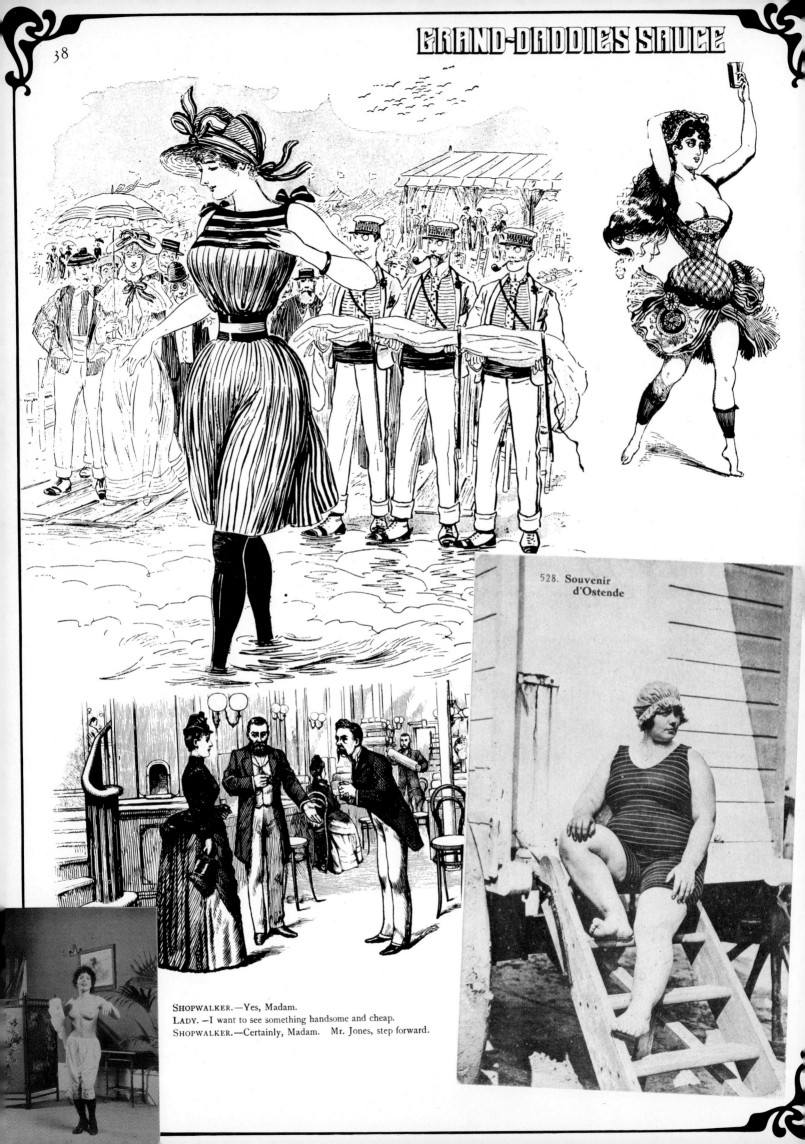

528. Souvenir d'Ostende

SHOPWALKER.—Yes, Madam.
LADY. —I want to see something handsome and cheap.
SHOPWALKER.—Certainly, Madam.   Mr. Jones, step forward.

"It gets frightfully crowded. I think this place would be more popular if not so many people came here."

"My Jack got run over last week, right
outside the hospital."
"Well, I never! He always was lucky."

Famous Songs. No. 14
"Pale Hands I Loved . .

"He be waiting for the next train. What he don't know is, the next train's gone."

"The treasures of the deep"

PUNCH

Old Lady: Come on, boy—be polite. Get up
    and give one of those young ladies a seat.
   Boy: Why don't *you* get up, and give them *both* a seat?

Ma: I bet you'd rather be sitting next to
    a gentleman, wouldn't you?
Swell: Yes, I would.
Ma: Yerse—me too.

Model: Do hurry up, Mister O'Brian—isn't the pose right yet?
Artist: Yes, yes, you look just right now. It's a beautiful
    picture. Come round and have a look at it.

PUNCH

PUNCH

Motor-car Driver: Get out of the way!
Victim: Why, are you coming back?

The young master: Eggs again, Mary?
    Can't you get the hens to lay
    something else?

WHO IS IT? AH! IT'S DEAR MAMA!

A GOOD ALL-ROUNDER
No wonder all the other girls
Call me all sorts of names.
I'm dutiful, and beautiful,
And *wonderful* at games.

GRAND-DADDIES SAUCE

Gent: Are the sandwiches fresh, my boy?
Country Youth: Don't know, I'm sure, sir. I've only been here a fortnight.

Small Girl (staring): Mummy—is that all *one lady?*

THE EMANCIPATION OF THE SKIRT.

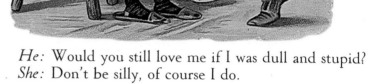

He: Would you still love me if I was dull and stupid?
She: Don't be silly, of course I do.

He: Well, are we to marry, or not?
She: I shan't—you do as you like.

He: I'll take you on a round-the-world tour.
She: Oh. Can't we go somewhere else?

She: There are lots of girls who don't wish to marry.
He: I know—I've proposed to most of them.

Eyeglass: My brother had a spot of bad luck. Horse trod on his face.
Whiskers: Was he hurt?
Eyeglass: No—improved his looks no end.

Golden-Haired Siren: The curate put his arm round me three times last night.
Dark-Eyed Beauty: He must have a very long arm.

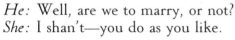

AN ALPHABET OF BEAUTY

A is for Anna (for short, Annabella)

B is for Betty, who's short of a feller

C is for Charity, always deserving

D is for Dulcie, with fervour unnerving

E is for Emma, who looks like a man

F is for Fanny, seen here with her fan

G is for Gwen, who lives down by the mill

H is for Hannah, who's over the hill

I is for Isabel, tops in her class

J is for Jennie, an absolute ass.

K is for Kathleen, who wears only beads

L is for Lucy, a stoker from Leeds

M is for Mary, who cannot keep still

N is for Nora, who hopes that you will

O is for Olive, who wears a long shawl

P is for Pat, who sticks hers on the wall

Q is for Queenie, quite regal she sits

R is for Rose—she has very sharp wits

S is for Sue, with her striptease so neat

T is for Tess, with the large country seat.

UVWXYZ, are all fully covered by Brenda in bed!

THE GIRL ON A BOX OF CIGARS

The girls of the East, and the girls of the West
Be they titled princesses, or chars—
I dote on them all; but the girl I love best
Is the Girl on a box of cigars.

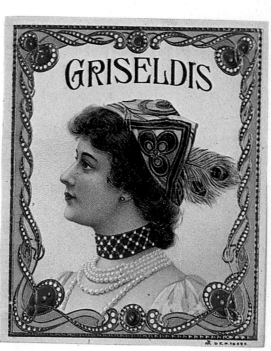

How elusive she is—she's not seen in the street
You don't find her in shops or bazaars—
My life-long ambition is one day to meet
The Girl on a box of cigars.

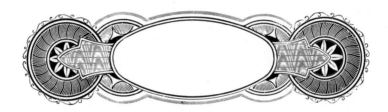

I've tried looking in restaurants, cafés, and such;
I've searched in bordellos and bars.
But I've never yet found one I like half as much
As the Girl on a box of cigars.

Oh that smile—angel-sweet! How those lips do entreat!
Oh those eyes, how they shimmer like stars!
Is she copied from life? Is she somebody's wife,
That Girl on the box of cigars?

She assumes many guises—an Indian maid,
Or a goddess, stepped down from a vase;
A huntress, a temptress, a mistress, a mate—
That's the Girl on a box of cigars!

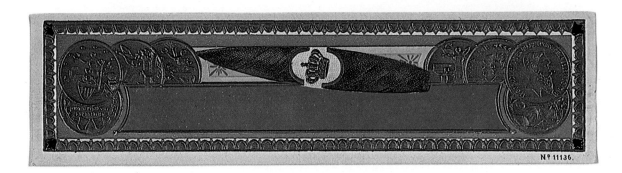

On some far distant shores, behind bolted doors,
She is feasted and fêted by Shahs;
Or in Austrian spas, in remote cable-cars,
By young mashers with Heidelberg scars;

Or by young Lochinvars who've come out of the West
Or Frenchmen with sly Ooh-la-la's—
Or Jolly Jack Tars with hair on their chest
Or magnificent mounted Hussars.

But no!—the Earth's sphere can't contain her, I fear—
And her home must be Venus, or Mars.
What hope then have I, of "giving the eye"
To the Girl on a box of cigars?

But I'll still smoke my smoke, and I'll praise to the skies
With a chorus of rousing hurrahs
That sweet, unattainable goddess—the Girl
On a box of street-corner cigars.

Nº 11198.

52

H.M.S. Victory. Here Nelson Fell

She leans against the sheaf of corn,
She was so glad to find it—
She rests content, all passion spent—
    And this is the lad behind it.

Captain (indicating plaque on floor):
    Here is where Nelson fell, your
    majesty.
King Edward VII: I'm not surprised.
    I nearly tripped over the damn
    thing myself.

When I was but a lad I learned
That there were Graces Three;
One was Faith, another Hope,
The other, Charity.
I went and saw the marble group
That came from Italy—
A pale cold Faith,
a lifeless Hope
A stony Charity.

Then later on, at Father's club,
(One evening, after tea)
I saw another version that
Seemed much more real to me
They hung there in the
            billiard-room
For all the world to see—
A far more life-like picture of
Faith, Hope and Charity.

And as I grew, I still
        pursued
My constant thirst for
        knowledge
To Oxford University,
To dear Old Keble
        College.
'Twas there I met the
        final set
I never have forgot 'em—
Gracie Jones and
        Gracie Smith.
And Gracie
        Higginbottom.

SAUCE PIQUANTE

REGRETFULLY no prizes are being offered for the sauciest picture in the book, but whichever way you look at it (and there is plenty of choice) the one on this page must be in the running (and I'm not referring to the Eiffel Tower).

The French artist, above all, seems to be able to capture that certain look, that particular stance, that tilt of the chin, even that glint in the eye, which charms and amuses the spectator.

Some of the jokes in the following section have been translated, somewhat loosely, into a more acceptable English form; others are just as they were. Most of the pictures don't even have captions, they speak for themselves.
But in what delightful accents!

"Fashion"

is a luxury we cannot afford," says this French demoiselle in an Edwardian magazine. "How about dressing in newspaper? With this magnifying glass, it's easy to read between the lines."

Plus de bijoux!

Plus de fards, plus de parfums, plus de poudre!

Plus de corset (on en portait déjà si peu!)

Plus de bas de soie!

Plus de fines chemises de linon!

Et à quoi bon un miroir!

Mais la femme elle-même n'est-elle pas un objet de luxe des plus coûteux?

"No more jewellery, perfumes, or powders; No more corsets—"

"No more stockings or chemises (and what's the good of a mirror?). In fact, the only luxury we can afford is Woman."

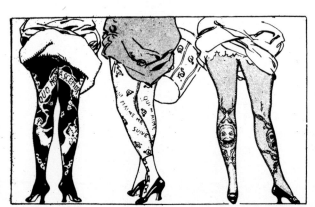

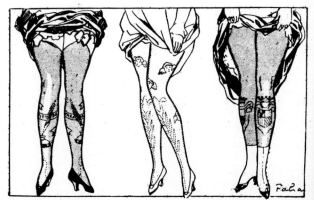

(How about leg-painting?)

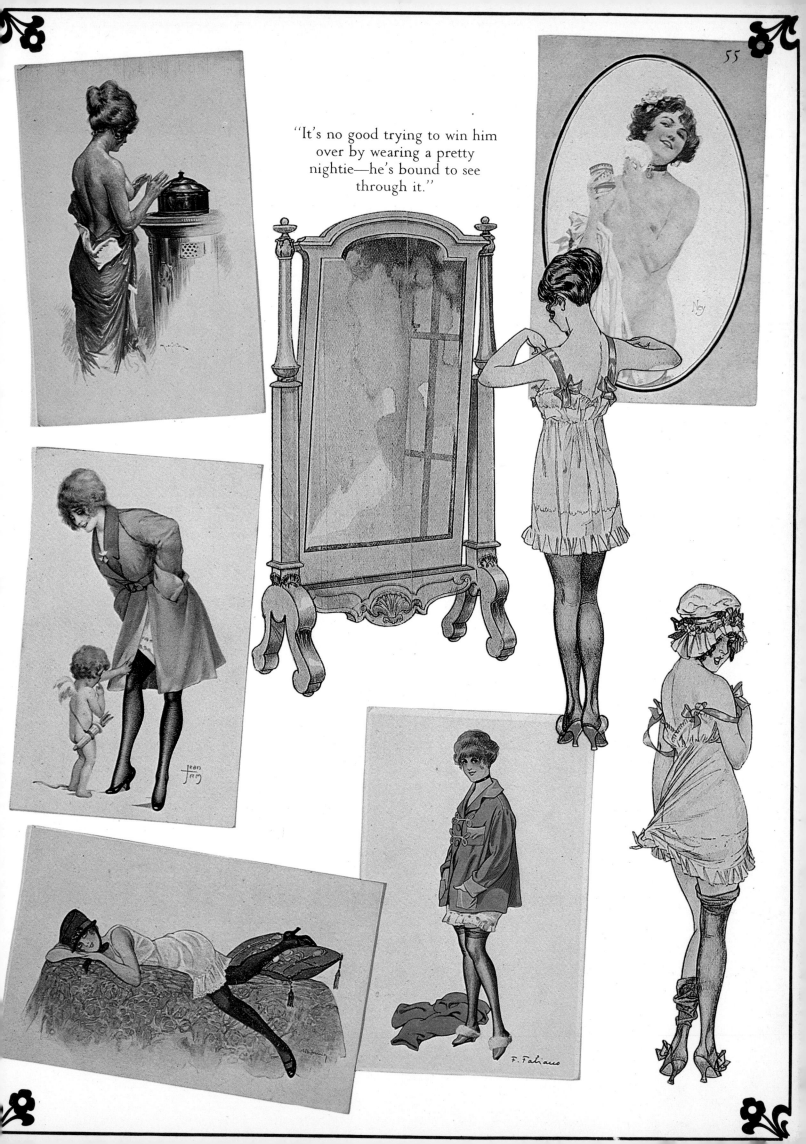

"It's no good trying to win him over by wearing a pretty nightie—he's bound to see through it."

SAUCE PIQUANTE

Fashion and the weather

The Paris Girl in Winter (dressed for cocktails at six)

"It's the eternal 'weather' problem—weather I can afford it or not."

The Paris Girl in Summer (dressed for tennis at two)

Avez-vous le vent debout? *Protégez votre dos...* *Par la tempête: Restez chez vous et... invitez-moi.* *Et par un Temps de bourrasque Mon Dieu... soignez vos dessous!*

"Don't go out and be blown about —stay at home (and invite me)"

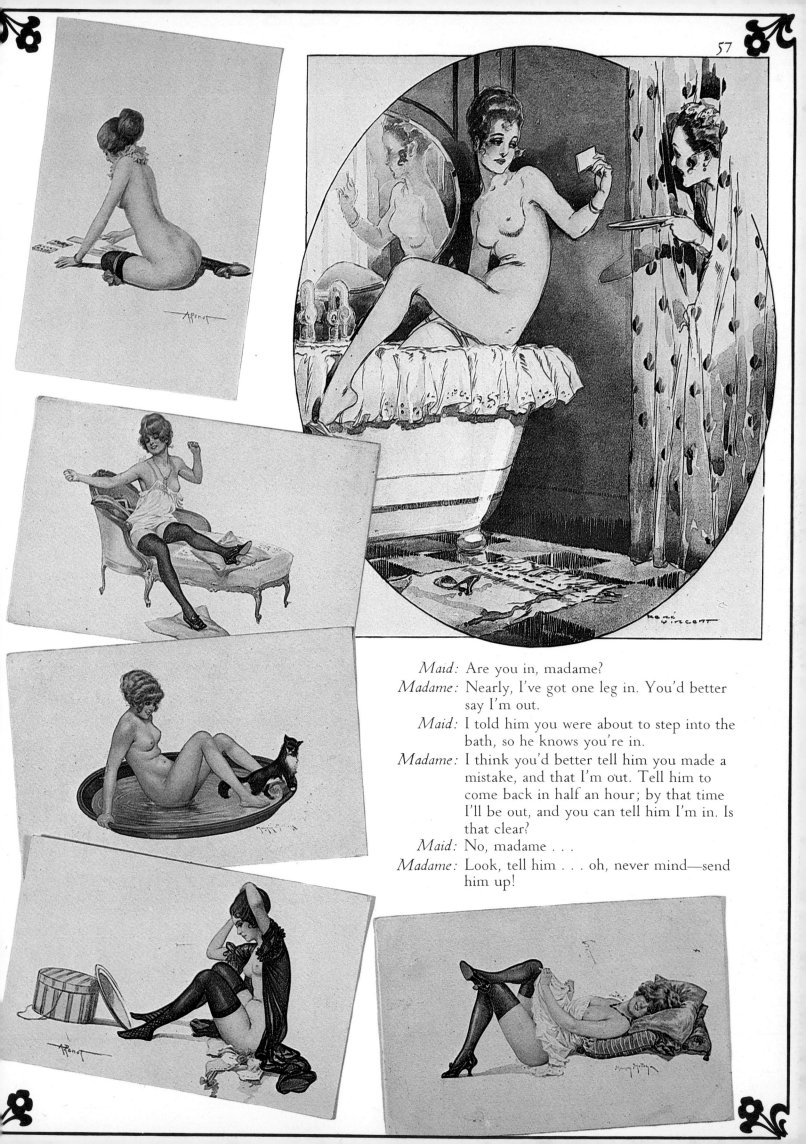

Maid: Are you in, madame?

Madame: Nearly, I've got one leg in. You'd better say I'm out.

Maid: I told him you were about to step into the bath, so he knows you're in.

Madame: I think you'd better tell him you made a mistake, and that I'm out. Tell him to come back in half an hour; by that time I'll be out, and you can tell him I'm in. Is that clear?

Maid: No, madame . . .

Madame: Look, tell him . . . oh, never mind—send him up!

SAUCE PIQUANTE

"Just what the doctor ordered"

Patient: Is that anything to worry about, doctor, that heart thumping?

Doctor: Not really—it's mine!

"I come to you with heavy heart" (Molière)

A.: How long have you been coming to this surgery?

B.: Three years.

A.: Have you *always* had to take all your clothes off, whatever the reason for your visit?

B.: Yes; but it's worth it. He's a *very* good dentist.

Doctor: I'm afraid I can find nothing wrong with you, madame. Quite frankly, I think it's due to drink.

Patient: In that case, doctor, you'd better come back when you're sober.

"Would you please just check me over once again doctor—there may be a couple of small points you have overlooked."

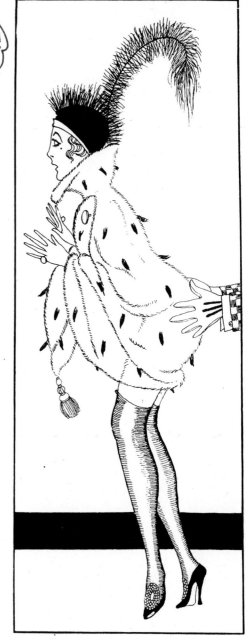

A huntsman, unseen,
uses methods unfair
Persuading the fox to abandon
its lair.

It's not often you see one of these
on the loose
It's a fine-looking, old-fashioned,
fur-covered goose.

The copy-cat

She: I've joined the fur
and feathered
league.

He: Is that the uniform?
Where are the
feathers?

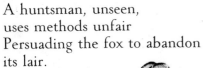

SAUCE PIQUANTE

Xmas is coming,
The goose is getting fat
Please put a penny
In the Old Man's hat.

Mistletoe is going up,
Though the price is shocking,
She's got enough to fill
An Old Man's stocking.

Summer Love may inflame the
heart, and warmth to the
blood may spring
But roaring heat of a Winter's
fire warms every little thing.

"BALD HEAD" ROW.

U.S. 726

SAUCE PIQUANTE

Finally, French girls as portrayed by Parisian artists
just about ten years before Toulouse Lautrec and
his beloved Moulin Rouge.

SAUCE OF THE NILE

An Arabian night, and a Turkish Delight,
And the Sphinx's inscrutable smile
And the girl who'll be back in a couple of sheiks—
That's what's known as the Sauce of the Nile.

When buying wives, Sheik Ali Khat
Prefers them plump and whopping
His constant motto: "Buy in Bulk—
It saves last-minute shopping."

LIFE IN THE HAREM: The dream...   ...and the reality

MAIN LINE

Engaged!

When I sit in railway carriages, I often think of all the marriages
Whose first few blissful moments are realised in the dining car;
Or rattling out of London Town, snugly with the shutters down.
Steaming down to Bracing Brighton, steaming down without the light on,
Realising, none too soon, "George, we're on our honeymoon!"
Full of eagerness and dread—wondering what lies ahead;
Can we cope, make both ends meet? Pull together? Find our feet?
Will she soon get tired of me? Do we face monotony?
Will he always buy me flowers? Was there ever love like ours?
How did fate conspire to match us?
　　　　　　　Will the guard come in and catch us?

"THE WEDDING DAY."

"Joy ATTEND on you and BLISSFUL HOURS lie before you."

All tickets please!

ALL SORTS

Off for a week at the seaside—
Oh, what a jolly affair!
Off for a pint, and a paddle—
All sorts of folk will be there.
Last year I stayed at Miss Knocker's;
Really, the food was a *crime*—
Sausages, all shapes and sizes
That's what she served all the time.

There were: small ones, tall ones, rolled up in a ball ones,
Long ones, strong ones, horrible and high,
Pale ones, frail ones, thereby-hangs-a-tale ones,
Red ones, dead ones, and ones that wouldn't die.
Edible, treadable, some that were incredible,
Bashed ones, mashed ones—not a pretty sight.
Tangled, mangled, very nearly strangled,
Washed ones, squashed ones, you got 'em every night.

Pavilion and Parade, Rhyl

I'd like to go halves in that.

THE MORE I TOOK, THE MORE I WANTED

I saw this near Southampton the other Day.
Was it You?

Out for a blow in the evening—
Stroll down the "Prom" after dark
Down past the pier, and the lighthouse
Then take a turn round the park;
They say all the world loves a lover,
In the park that is certainly true—
They are so busy loving each other
That you've hardly got room to get through!

There are slim ones, grim ones, pretty
little prim ones,
Shy ones, sly ones, fancy ones and plain,
Rough ones, tough ones, cannot get
enough ones,
Some who hadn't been before, and
wouldn't come again.

Squat ones, hot ones, give-me-all-
you've-got ones,
Game ones, tame ones, putting up a fight—
Vast ones, fast ones, try to make it last ones,
Everybody spooning on a moonlit night!

(continued)

LOVE DIVINE
Can love be sweeter with its bliss,   A kiss of love, 'tis but the truth,
When such a chance occurs like this?   Is but the vital spark of youth,

" I find things looking up."

A bit of alright.

Ostende
Type de Baigneuse

OSTENDE. - Baigneuses

ALL SORTS

Down for a dip in the briny!
Laughing and splashing about,
Watching the girls in the water—
Waiting for them to come out;
Stroll past the back of a beach-hut
Glimpsing the ladies behind;
All in their best bathing-dresses,
Each one a different kind—

(continued)

Click went the Kodak.

Baigneuse

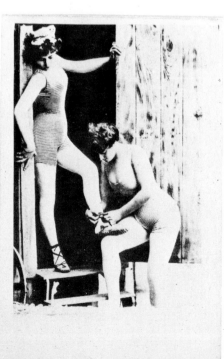

J. T. W & Co. 6.

WE ARE SPENDING EVERY HOUR OF THE DAY
BY THE SEA IN THIS DELIGHTFUL WAY

Ser. Aqua No. 126

ALL SORTS

There are green ones, lean ones,
stringy runner-bean ones,
Black ones, slack ones, barrels and
balloons,
Fat ones, flat ones, welcome-on-the
mat ones,
Tiny little orange ones, and big
full moons.
Square ones, bare ones, toss 'em in
the air ones,
Bright ones, tight ones, lollipops
and lumps;
Town ones, brown ones, wobbling up
and down ones,
Dainty little spotted ones, and great
big bumps.

It takes all sorts to make a world
Or so they always say—
And down by the sea all sorts
you'll see
On a seaside holiday!

LA MER & SON PUBLIC, par Mars.
— Simple reflexion, madame, si j'ose me permettre: Vous ne craignez pas de les
enrhumer, à la fenêtre ouverte?

THERE'S EVER SUCH A LOT
OF PRETTY SPOTS ROUND HERE

SAUCE ON THE FORCE

Though a policeman's lot is not, traditionally, a happy one, other people have always found his "lot" a subject for amusement. In the days of below-stairs servants' quarters, he was usually to be found in the company of the kitchen maids, who never stopped feeding him, or so we are led to believe, with steaming meat-pies, legs of lamb and jugs of beer. The cook was constantly being surprised by the mistress of the house, while in the arms of Bobby, the Boy in Blue. This was, of course, in the days when there were hardly any traffic problems, due to the fact that there was hardly any traffic. The upholder of law and order could therefore be excused the occasional lapse he succumbed to, spell it how you will.

Bobby's Pet.

NOW THEN COME OUT OF IT, OR I'LL PINCH YER CLOTHES.

Bobby: What are you doing?
Boy: Nothing.
Bobby: Why?
Boy: It's all I could think to do.
Bobby: Ah. Er—well—don't let me
 catch you doing it again.

I apprehend the
 parlourmaid
I will not set her free
I grab her by the
 bushes
And that's where she
 grabs me.

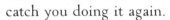

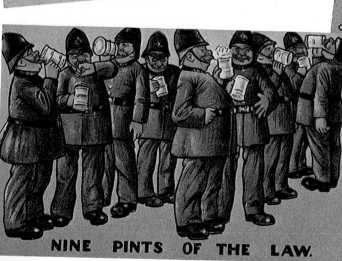

NINE PINTS OF THE LAW.

"MARY, I THOUGHT I HEARD A MAN'S VOICE !!"
"MUST HAVE COME FROM THE FLAT UNDERNEATH, SIR !!"

SAUCE ON THE FORCE

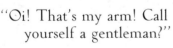

1. Salute the British Policewoman
   In every kind of weather
   Her chest flung out, her head
       thrown back
   Her knees stuck close together
   I sit behind her all day long
   You don't hear me complaining—
   Can *you* think of a better place
   To go when it is raining?

2. I've got to know her very well
   (Admiring her intensely)
   And though I'm just a doggie, I
   Look up to her immensely.
   And when she turns and smiles
       at me
   It makes my whiskers bristle
   I know her voice, I know her name
   And where she keeps her whistle.

"Building up the Force"

UNDER POLICE PROTECTION.

"Have you the time, officer?"
"I have, miss, if you have."

"Oi! That's my arm! Call
   yourself a gentleman?"

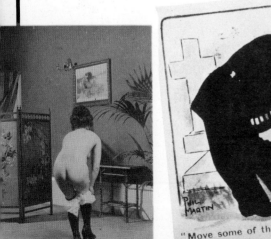

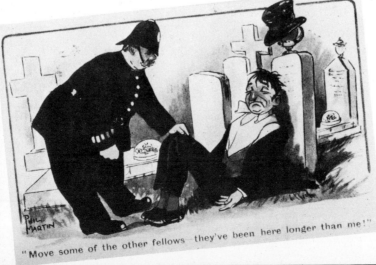

"Move some of the other fellows they've been here longer than me!"

3. Though puppy-dogs are known
       for their
   Impulsive natural actions
   And dirty dogs behave so much
   More vulgarly than fractions
   If she cares to share the shelter that
   Her uniform affords her
   There is nothing I can do except
   Reciprocate towards her.
(. . . and he did—all over her leg.)

ONLY TO SEE HER FACE AGAIN!

Exceeding the Limits.

I COULD GET ON A.1.,

IF YOU'LL SEND ME PLENTY OF COPPERS.

ORL RIGHT Mr PLICEMAN I AM SEEING HIM HOME

BELATED TRAVELLER.
"Shay Old Chap can (hic) you tell me the (hic) nearest way out of this Forest."

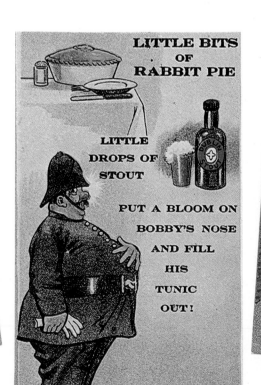

LITTLE BITS OF RABBIT PIE

LITTLE DROPS OF STOUT

PUT A BLOOM ON BOBBY'S NOSE AND FILL HIS TUNIC OUT!

IS IT TRUE YOU'RE ENGAGED, OR IS IT A FORCE OF HABIT?

"NOT TOO TALL AND

(Words by Albert Clegg / Music by Harold Miller)

Sung with great success in most halls by George Tilley

VERSE ONE

I havn't been out with a girl for years, now maybe you think I'm slow:
No, that's not the reason, I'll tell you why: I'm particular, you know.
Some girls are two a penny, and others a halfpenny each—
I don't want them; the girl I seek, must be a perfect peach—

CHORUS

Not too tall and not too short, not too thick or thin—
She must come out where she should come out and go in where she
    should go in—
She mustn't have much too much behind, or much too little in front—
If ever I have a girl again, that's the girl I want.

VERSE TWO

I heard about a girl called May, she sounded quite a catch—
"She's only five foot five," they said, "with golden hair to match."
But when I met her in the woods I knew I'd been sold a pup.
'Cos she was taller lying down than when she was standing up!

ΠΟΤ ΤΟΟ SHORT "

(REPEAT CHORUS—Not too tall, etc.)

VERSE THREE
Then I met Rachel Rosenbloom, an Irish girl from Wales
She had a face like a summer's morn, and a shape like a bag of nails;
"Could I only see your face," I said, "I never more would roam—
So bring your dear sweet face to me, and leave your body at home!"

(REPEAT CHORUS—Not too tall, etc.)

LAST VERSE
At last I met my heart's desire, a girl called Annie More
She walked in beauty as the night—with legs right down to the floor.
I pressed my suit, she creased her frock, we had a splendid spree—
She was the girl I was looking for—now her husband is looking for me!

(REPEAT CHORUS—Not too tall, etc.)

THE HAT

Ask any woman
She'll promise you that
The thing that she loves to
Wear most is a hat.

She may be more shop-girl
Than aristocrat
She'll always look upper-
Crust wearing a hat.

If her corset collapses
And she's feeling flat
She'll perk up no end if
You buy her a hat.

In chemise she may pose
Or sit nude on the mat
She'll always look dressed when
She's wearing a hat.

Though her chin is too long
And her legs are too fat
She'll think herself beautiful
Dressed in a hat.

"Ooh, My Hat!!"

WHO CARES FOR RAIN!

And however absurd
Be a true diplomat
And *always* enthuse with
Regard to her hat.

Up and down she'll cavort
Like a French acrobat
And she'll bend over backwards
To please, after that.

And be warned—she may suddenly
Spit like a cat
In the street, "Ooh, the harlot!
She's wearing my hat!!"

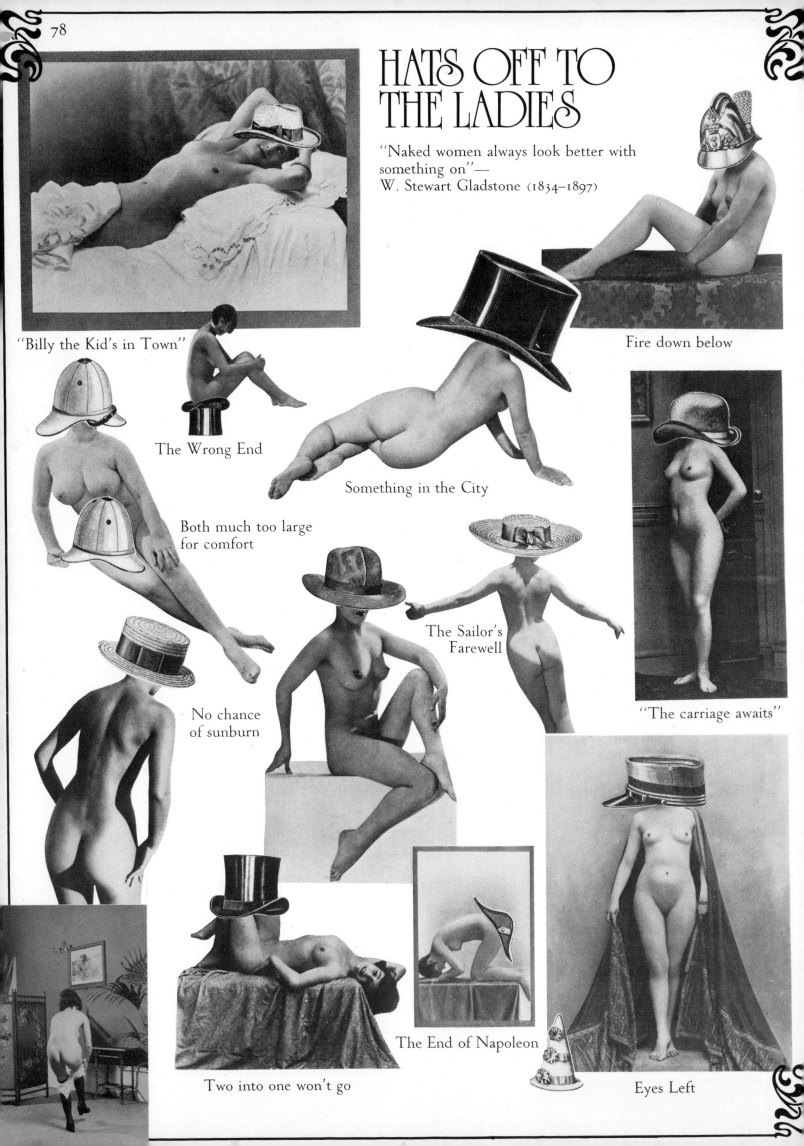

HATS OFF TO THE LADIES

"Naked women always look better with something on"—
W. Stewart Gladstone (1834–1897)

"Billy the Kid's in Town"

Fire down below

The Wrong End

Something in the City

Both much too large for comfort

The Sailor's Farewell

"The carriage awaits"

No chance of sunburn

The End of Napoleon

Two into one won't go

Eyes Left

MIXED DOUBLES
(or matched pairs)

I'm known as being quite a sport
And game for any game;
And 'though I play all sorts of
    things
I'm careful, just the same—

You may not think it cricket, but
I need your promise true—
You promise to play ball with me
Then I'll play ball with you.

I bought myself
Some purple shoes
In Kensington
Arcade
But now I find
I have no dress
To match their
Violent shade
So unlike Cinderella
I *shan't* go to the Ball—
If I can't wear my purple shoes
I won't go out at all.

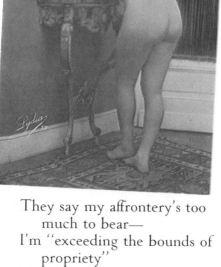

I stand in the hall with no
    callers at all
I really don't know who's the
    rudest;
I say it's them, and *they* say
    it's me
(For becoming a practising
    Nudist).

They say my affrontery's too
    much to bear—
I'm "exceeding the bounds of
    propriety"
If that is the case then the
    answer is clear—
I'll just turn my back on society.

WORCESTERSHIRE SAUCE

How it got its name

Worcestershire Sauce, so the story goes, was not originally made in Worcestershire at all, but in Hornsey. When it was first sold to the public, it was therefore called Hornsey Sauce. As soon as it was put on the market, it began to sell like hot cakes, but after the public found that it didn't have any, shall we say, medicinal properties, and was merely a sauce, business dropped off considerably.

The inventor, Mr. Joseph Harris, sat in his empty restaurant in Hornsey.

He was desperately trying to conjure up a change of name for his product—one that would suggest the spicy, countryfied, fresh-air taste of the stuff, when in walked a young Negro, fresh from the docks at the Port of London, and ordered one of the tenpenny hot dinners that were advertised in the restaurant window.

Joseph Harris owes his vast wealth to that moment in time. For the Negro docker, his tenpenny meal steaming in front of him, picked up the bottle of sauce from the table, stared at it, and said "Wha's dis here sauce?"—and that is what it has been called ever since.

London Opinion

The Sea-(in)-side smile.

TONGUE-TWISTER DEPARTMENT

(Say this six times:–)

See that sauce-box on the sea-shore; in her scanty silk swimsuit and stockings. She has split the side of her swimsuit, so she says, and has sewn it up with strong thick string. Strong thick string isn't suitable for sewing up the sides of split swimsuits as we can see, because these sauce-boxes are showing their skin through the sides.

Should any sailors sauntering on the sea-shore spot these slits in the sides of their scanty silk swimsuits, these two sauce-boxes might, in certain circumstances, suddenly find themselves in a similar state to, if not a sauce-box, then certainly a sauce-bottle—tipped upside down and shaken.

SAUCES IN THE FORCES

Welcome Home
(five different ways)

He: Dulcie!
She: Jack!
He: I'm Geoffrey, actually . . .
She: Yes, well, as a matter of fact, I'm Mabel, but don't let *that* stand in our way!

She: Oh, I'm so happy; it can't last. Mark my words, there'll be tears before bedtime.
He: Really! They'll have to start pretty soon.

Manoeuvres

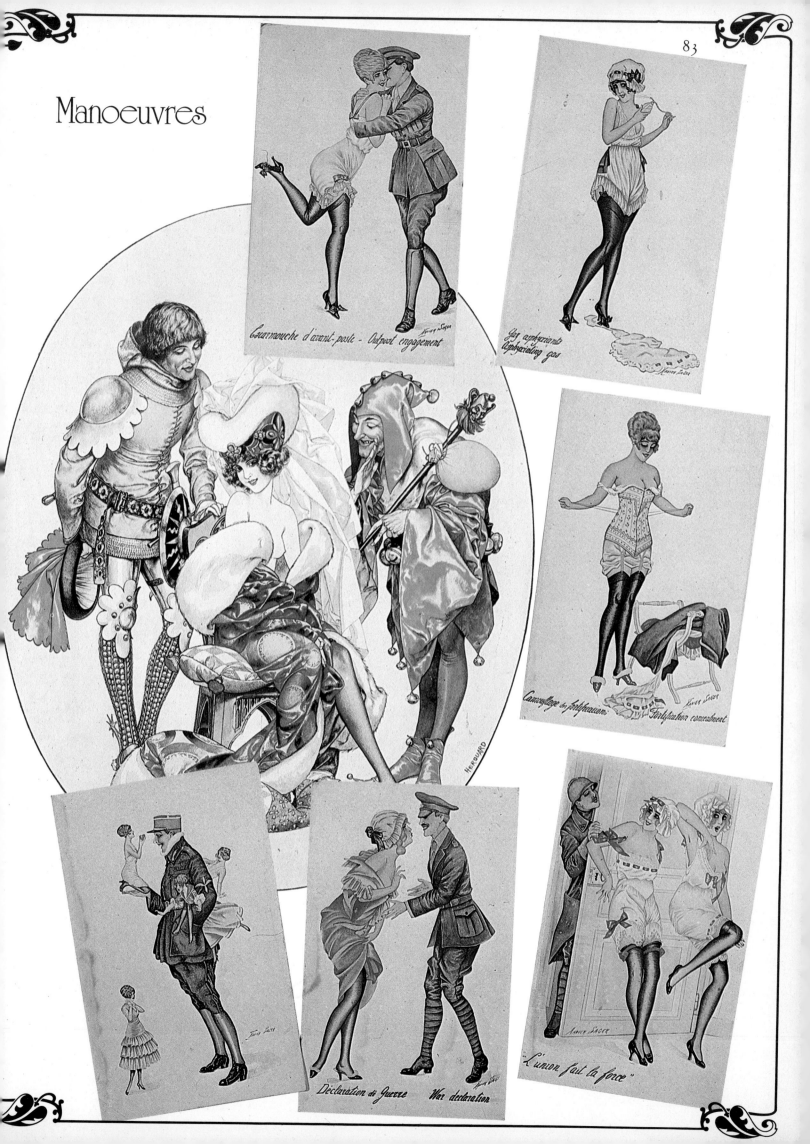

Escarmouche d'avant-poste – Outpost engagement

Gaz asphyxiants – Asphyxiating gas

Camouflage des fortifications – Fortification concealment

Déclaration de Guerre – War declaration

"L'union fait la force"

HÉROUARD

"The Informer"

General: "And what were you doing, my man, when you started this war?"
Tommy: "Oo said I started this blinkin war?"

She: When are you going back to the front?
He: As soon as I've finished undoing this bit at the back!

"The Apparition"

"My boy's been out there twelve months without a scratch."
"Good heavens! what insect powder does he use?"

LYRIC THEATRE

SAUCE ON THE BOARDS

LONDON NIGHT-LIFE was inextricably bound up with the Music Halls; and the Music Halls were, unquestionably, the place for sauce. If you wanted a bit of sauce, that's where you went of an evening, and if you didn't get it from the stage, you got it from the audience. The atmosphere engendered it—the gilt, gaudy auditorium, the over-painted girls, the over-lit, over-heated, over-crowded hall seemed to create the excitement associated with the now-or-never feeling pervading the place. People plucked up their courage, perhaps fortified with a little Scottish wine, and actually answered the comic back; the gentlemen crowding the pit cheered on the ladies who danced, encouraging them to twirl a little faster, to kick a little higher; and these ladies, swept up and carried along by the waves of applause, complied in the main, with the gentlemen's requests. The important thing was that everyone clapped and sang, and laughed and cheered—and when they left, and poured out into the cold night, they took with them sore throats, stinging palms, and memories of a joyous evening which they themselves had helped to create.

Not at all like television.

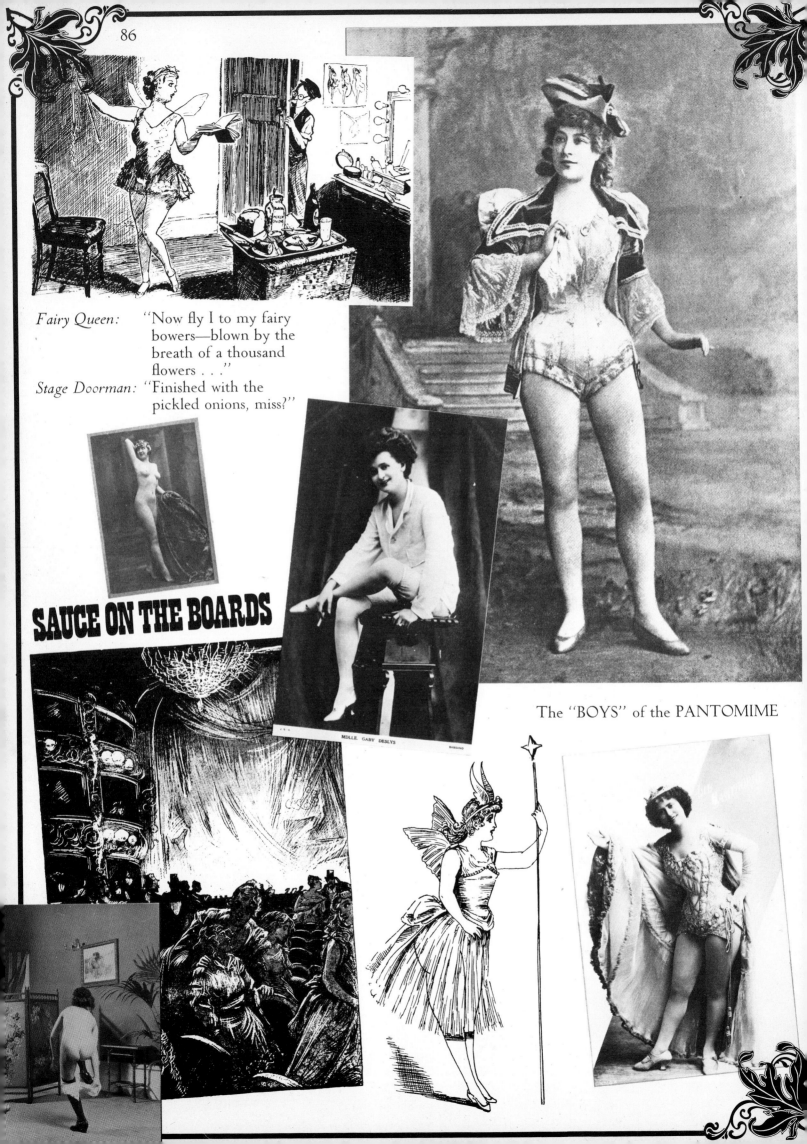

Fairy Queen: "Now fly I to my fairy bowers—blown by the breath of a thousand flowers . . ."

Stage Doorman: "Finished with the pickled onions, miss?"

SAUCE ON THE BOARDS

MDLLE. GABY DESLYS

The "BOYS" of the PANTOMIME

THE LONDON PAVILION.

PICCADILLY, W.

We come every night and we sit in the
    gallery
Armed with tomatoes and eggs.
We're none of us posh, but we know what
    we like—
And we do like a nice pair of legs!

CANCAN
1.
ENTRÉE.

"IF MY GAL GETS TO KNOW OF THIS IT'S
ALL OVER BETWEEN US!"

Fighting over their "lines".

SAUCE ON THE BOARDS A peep behind the scenes....

"Is it all right, Gladys? Do you need something to copy from?"
"I've got something to copy from, only it's upside down!"

ENCOURAGEMENT.

ROSY (*her first appearance*).—I feel awfully queer in these things. Shall fancy everybody's staring at me.
BABY.—Oh, nonsense; don't you worry about that. I'm always on when you are, you know.

Diplomatic stage-hand (who has entered the wrong dressing-room): "Beg pardon, gentlemen—I thought this was the Ladies' Room."

HURRY UP AND JOIN US

Miss Madge Lessing

4006 E ROTARY PHOTO, E.C. MISS MARGARET RUBY.

MARY WAS A DRESSMAKER,
BUT SHE COULDN'T MAKE IT PAY —
SO SHE WENT UPON THE STAGE —
"THINGS ARE LOOKING UP," THEY SAY!

Whenever I go out, You can hear the people shout, "Get yer 'air cut!"

REVELATIONS OF A SOCIETY ACTRESS

LEAVES A VERY LITTLE TO THE IMAGINATION

Two brothers went upon the boards
But brother acts were a penny for ten
So they started up a sister act.
But dressed themselves like *smart
young men*.
The act caught on. Sustained applause
And cheers would greet their entry.
They're both now dowager
Duchesses,
'Cos they married into the Gentry.

SAUCE ON THE BOARDS

A SUGGESTION TO THE REFRESHMENT DEPARTMENTS OF OUR THEATRES.

How to get Fat!!

Buy it of your Butcher like Decent People :: ::

THE FOLLIES

MAY BE ENGAGED FOR

Balloon Ascents,
Shareholders Meetings,
Army Manœuvres,
Jam Making,
Clapham Junction,
or any other form of
Light Social
Entertainment

For Vacant Dates, Figs, Nuts and Bananas, write enclosing Postal Order 21/-

IVE-A-CORN The DASTIEST TAINTIEST

Preparation of Prepared Meat Juice ever prepared from Wood Shavings Direct. In Four Flavours

Onion, Rose, Mud, Dubbin, Flotsam, Jetsam, Fondstool

Ask for it at the Bar! You won't get it!

REFRESHMENTS

Penny Bun	✱✱✱✱✱	
Sandwiches, Assorted (Fishpaste, Toothpaste, (Carbolic or Chickweed) Single 1d. Return 2½d.		2d.
Cake, Slice of		
Luck, Slice of		1d.
Bank Rate		1d.
Ninepence	per cent.	3½
		4d.

EDWARD'S STARLEINE

FOR THE FAIR

MAKES THE FAT, FIT AND THE FIT, FAT

REID

THIS CAREFULLY

A Retired Fair One, writes—" I cannot tell you the good your Starleine has done me as I have never tried it."

Are your Boots too long:

WADHAM

QUEERSON* LATEST BOOKS

(*of "Queerson's Weekly.")

"How I Burst the Thermometer."

BY
HELENOR FLYNN

The Morning Post says—
The Sporting Times says—"We can't possibly do it Justice" ... Nothing

Try LAMBERT'S LAVENDER LOZENGES for LONELY LADIES

£1,000 FREE INSURANCE

is presented with this Programme

Against MUMPS,
CHICKEN-COUGH,
HOUSEMAID'S KNEE,
Or GRILLED SWEETBREADS

Sign here

If SANE, SOBER, or UNMARRIED

EMERGENCY EXIT

In case of Fire or Panic cut round the dotted line.

CUBHANAN'S
Whack and Bite Whisky

Try a Wine-Glass Full

Try Another
Try Another
Try Another
Try Another
Try Another

Try Another—Feel Better P—What P

CHEW NORA
"The Sign of Wealth"

GLOSSY GREEN
GOBBLING GLUE

Try it on your Friends

Hermetically seals the jaws and renders conversation abso. impos.

Show Business Maxims (No.38)

"If you can't make them laugh in the show,
Make them laugh in the interval" (by printing a funny programme).

THE FANCY BALL

Midnight air is shattered, scattered
   shrieks of laughter over all
Pink champagne is flowing; glowing
   Lanterns light the Fancy Ball.

Dancing limbs cavorting, sporting
   Garments that entrance, enthrall
Garter, boot, and stocking, shocking
   Emblems of the Fancy Ball.

Summer stars are twinkling, tinkling
   music makes its waterfall
Whispered words and glances, chances
   Taken at the Fancy Ball

Costumeless, I'm lying, sighing,
   Wondering what might befall
If I went sedately, stately,
   In my bear skin, to the Ball.

SAUCE ON THE BOARDS

Show Business Maxims (No 43)
"There's safety in numbers."

1hre La lecture des critiques

2hres La Toilette

4hres L'Interview du Courriériste Mondain

6hres Retour du bois

7hres L'Apéritif

8hres Chez le restaurateur

10hres En Scène

12hres Souper fin

Paris—Sept. 2nd, 1904

Dear Mum,

Just a line to let you know I have settled in nicely, and the show is going well. I have quite a nice lot of dancing to do and things in it. Don't they talk funny over here! Luckily Ivy speaks it, so when I'm with her I'm all right (which is not always).

I thought you'd like to know what a typical day is like. Well, yesterday for instance.

I didn't get up while nearly half-past one, as the first night had been late (or at least the goings-on afterwards). I've got good digs with a nice ~~double~~ big bed. I'm not wearing those nighties you made me as it's too hot. I bought a French one. It's got lace round the top and fur round the bottom. To keep my shoulders warm, Ivy says, but I don't know what she means.

At two o'clock I had a bath. There is a maid at the digs, who baths you and puts your clothes on. Then the landlord comes in and tries to take them off again. Only yesterday it wasn't the landlord, it was a gentleman from the press. That was at four. He didn't get anywhere, as I had to go out for a drive with Ivy. But there was a mix-up. When we met in the park, she'd come by bike, so we both went home again, as you can see on the card, at six p.m.

At seven, I met the Manager of the show—he had invited me to, as he said "partake of a pair o'teeth" with him. I didn't like the sound of it, but it was all right, it turned out to be just drinks. Then he asked me to "share his dinner" with him, but I said can we have one each, and he laughed at that. So, by ten o'clock we was doing the show. This is the Egyptian scene. I know the costumes don't look much, but the Manager says he can't afford lavish costumes like the big shows; and anyway, its not cold—you can feel the steam rising from the front row of the stalls. The only awkward moment is when we kneel and pray to the Sphinx—that's when the pea-shooters come out. But its all very artistic really.

After the show, I had supper with the Manager, but my feet were killing me so I didn't enjoy it much. After supper, we went ~~to his to my to~~ home. How's Dad and Tiddles? Write soon.

Your loving daughter,
Lily.

P.S. I may be getting a bigger part in the show, the Manager says. He says I deserve one. L.

(Words by George Sellars)

I CAN'T STAND BY, & JUST WATCH

VERSE ONE

I mingle a lot with society; I'm well known by the gentry, you
    see—
I often go round to Quaglino's; and *he* sometimes comes round
    to me.
I sat next to a beautiful lady, when I last went around there to sup;

'She was wearing a frightfully low-cut gown—
you could see she was well brought up:

She began to converse rather freely,
Her one pleasure, she said, was to cook—
She described what she did with her
    dumplings
'Til I didn't know which way to look.

Just then, an itinerant waiter
Dropped a large ice-cream right on
    her chest
As it slid out of sight she cried
    "Help me!
It's freezing! Oh, quick—
    do your best!"

CHORUS

Well I can't stand by and just watch others suffer
No, I have to go and try to make amends—
So I held her down by force
And applied hot chocolate sauce—
And ever since, we've both been bosom friends.

VERSE TWO

One night at the club I'd been drinking, and was staggering home,
    about three—
Well I'd missed all the cabs, and decided it was their turn to try
    missing me.
As I zig-zagged along the Embankment—(as I said, I'd had
    several halves),
On the bridge stood the butcher's young daughter, I could tell it
    was her by her calves.
She spoke in a disjointed fashion, "All the lights have gone out
    of my life,
I know it's not meet, but there's so much at stake, I shall chop out
    my heart with a knife."
I murmured, "That's tripe, you're a chump dear," ('twas the
    language she best understood)
She replied, "If I had but the guts, sir, I'd throw myself into the flood."

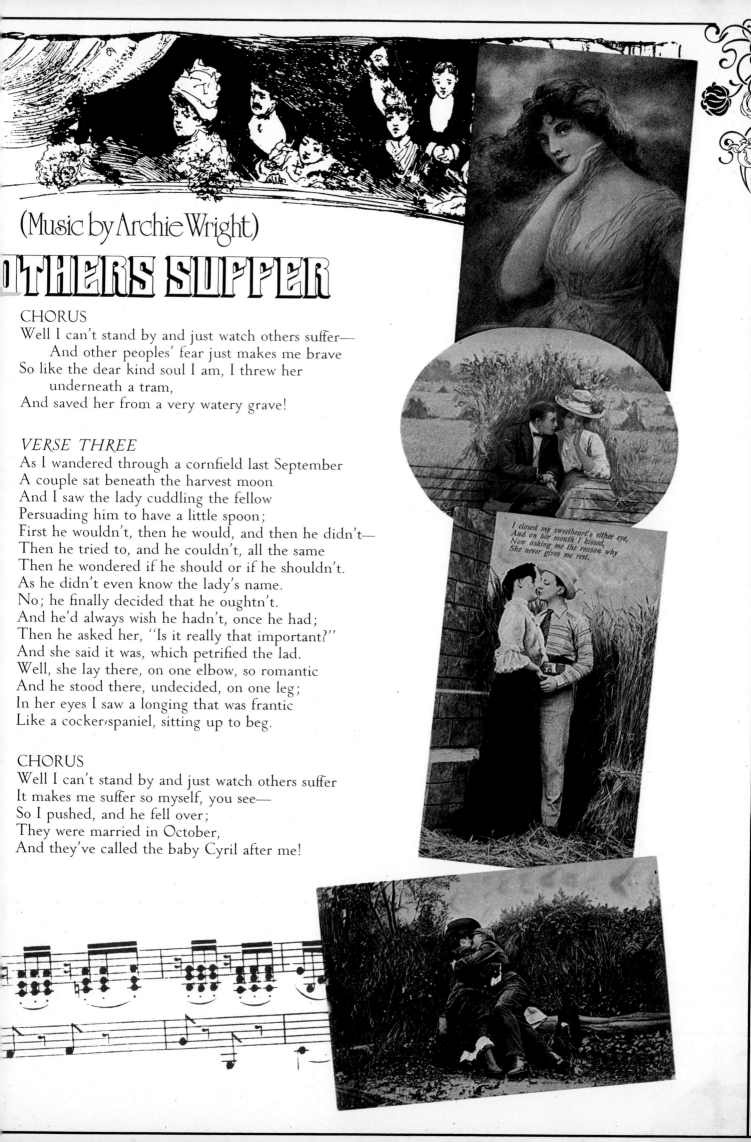

(Music by Archie Wright)

OTHERS SUFFER

CHORUS
Well I can't stand by and just watch others suffer—
   And other peoples' fear just makes me brave
So like the dear kind soul I am, I threw her
   underneath a tram,
And saved her from a very watery grave!

VERSE THREE
As I wandered through a cornfield last September
A couple sat beneath the harvest moon
And I saw the lady cuddling the fellow
Persuading him to have a little spoon;
First he wouldn't, then he would, and then he didn't—
Then he tried to, and he couldn't, all the same
Then he wondered if he should or if he shouldn't.
As he didn't even know the lady's name.
No; he finally decided that he oughtn't.
And he'd always wish he hadn't, once he had;
Then he asked her, "Is it really that important?"
And she said it was, which petrified the lad.
Well, she lay there, on one elbow, so romantic
And he stood there, undecided, on one leg;
In her eyes I saw a longing that was frantic
Like a cocker-spaniel, sitting up to beg.

CHORUS
Well I can't stand by and just watch others suffer
It makes me suffer so myself, you see—
So I pushed, and he fell over;
They were married in October,
And they've called the baby Cyril after me!

*I closed my sweetheart's either eye,
And on her mouth I kissed,
Now asking me the reason why
She never gives me rest.*

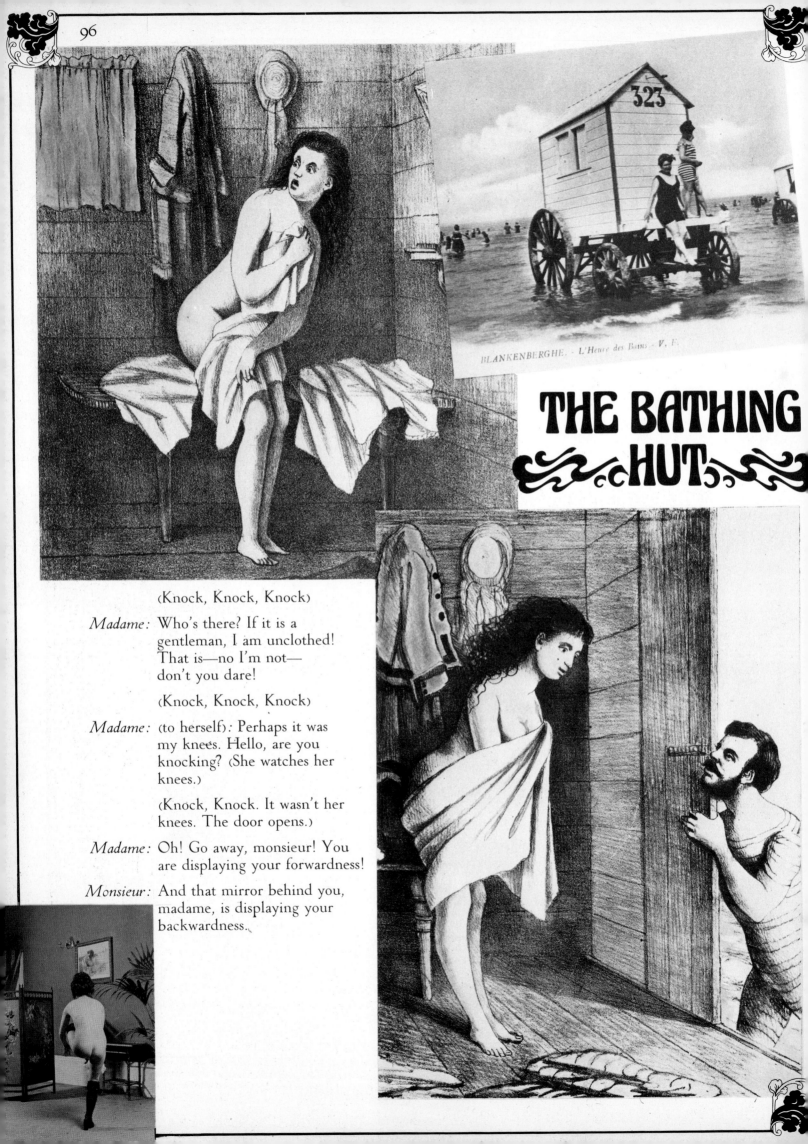

BLANKENBERGHE. - L'Heure des Bains - V. F.

THE BATHING HUT

(Knock, Knock, Knock)

Madame: Who's there? If it is a gentleman, I am unclothed! That is—no I'm not— don't you dare!

(Knock, Knock, Knock)

Madame: (to herself): Perhaps it was my knees. Hello, are you knocking? (She watches her knees.)

(Knock, Knock. It wasn't her knees. The door opens.)

Madame: Oh! Go away, monsieur! You are displaying your forwardness!

Monsieur: And that mirror behind you, madame, is displaying your backwardness.

THE FOLLOWER OF FORM

Top Girl: There's a man on the lawn, Janet. He's lying in the sun, without a stitch on.

Bottom Girl: Oo-er. Who is it?

Top Girl: It's the young master, with the *Daily Graphic* over his face.

Bottom Girl: How do you know?

Top Girl: I recognise the sporting section.

THE ORIGINAL DONALD McGILL

The opportunity to include some scribbles, and finished paintings, from the master of the saucy postcard was too good to be missed.

N.B. (Original pencil drawings and watercolours from the Author's collection.

"Please stop Johnny throwing stones at me. By the way, I believe I mentioned this before!"

"Shall we turn off the light and go to sleep?"
"Well, we'll turn off the light!"

Newly-Wed: "Have you got a dish two foot long and four inches wide?"
Shopkeeper: "What for, madam?"
Newly-Wed: "I want to make a rhubarb tart."

INSTABILITY
(of high heels) combined
with URGENCY, and
aided by
PONDEROSITY
(or heaviness)
resulting in the
subject showing her
VERSATILITY

SPINOSITY
(or pricklyness)
causing
SENSITIVITY
to the subjects
ROTUNDITY

CURIOSITY~possibly heading for
a certain amount FALLIBILITY

LAXITY
(or carelessness)
bringing about
a lack of
MODESTY,
and an increased
VISIBILITY

SAUCES OF EMBARRESSMENT

UNRELIABILITY
(of elastic) and the
PROBABILITY that
it will increase their
DROPABILITY

FAMILIARITY.
The ARTILLERY
taking advantage
of her
VULNERABILITY

VOLUMINOSITY (or fullness).
The Mushrooms of the March Wind;
dispelling VANITY,
but creating an air of FESTIVITY
and achieving immense
POPULARITY

DIRTY days hath September,
    April, June and November.
February's days are quite alright
(It only rains from morn till night).
All the rest have thirty-one
Without a blessed gleam of sun,
And if any of them had two-and-thirty
They'd be just as wet and just as dirty.

"That boy is staring at me.
I'll pull a face."

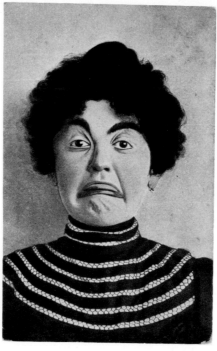

"I'll try looking nonchalant."

"Now I'll give him one of these."

(The boy returns the favour)

"Boo—he hates me!"

AT THE PALAIS

"Look at them two pulling funny
faces at each other, Bert."

EYE TEST CHART
do you need glasses?

1

1

If you cannot see this row, you are very shortsighted.

 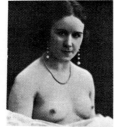  

If you cannot see this row, you are fairly shortsighted (or drunk).

Difficulty with this row is not uncommon.

This is the row for the average vision.

This is the bottom row.

These early puns, from one of the great purveyors of Victorian humour, Thomas Hood, lead us nicely into APPENDIX I (opposite)

A total eclipse of the sun

"Does your mother know you're out?"

Spade Husbandry

Best cure for a cold

Foot Soldiers

Held up to Ridicule

Appendix 1
Historical Section

Renovating old Jokes—bringing the sauce up to date.

I.........'m. rather Gapish !

Peeping back into the past, as the girl on the far left is doing (or at least she appears to be—it's possible, on the other hand, that she is merely waiting for the milkman to give her an extra one), is a tricky business.

There's nothing wrong in the actual peeping, but any deductions, drawn without expert knowledge, can be a chancy affair.

I have no expert knowledge of the origins of what we know as saucy humour; but of one thing I am certain—puns featured largely in its development. Thomas Hood loved them, as you may see on the opposite page; the Victorian and Edwardian postcard artists would have been lost without them. There could have been none of the jokes about Mary and her little bear behind, or concerning the lady whose enormous pear won first prize at the flower-show.

Early nineteenth-century humour seemed to lie in the illustration rather than the caption (the housemaid on the left, drawn about 1810, bears this out). But by the time *Punch* was first published, in the 1840s, written jokes were beginning to have more point and less padding—not so much fat, and a little more meat; and inevitably, the meat got nearer the knuckle. Sauce was on its way.

Puzzle: Find the apple of her eye.

It's a long lane that has no turning.

None but the brave deserve the fair.

The key to many a puzzle.

The Victorians loved puzzles—and these disguised proverbs are visual puns in themselves, either in the content of the picture, or in the relationship between the picture and its caption.

LOVE AND A COTTAGE.

The shape of a house, with handsome moustaches made out of creepers, and the shadow of a lady on the wall, showing her up in a rather unfavourable light, are a couple of good visual jokes poking fun at the fads and fashions of Mid-Victorian England; while in Germany, they too were having trouble with women's current obsession for protruding posteriors.

As always, those clever Germans have found a solution.

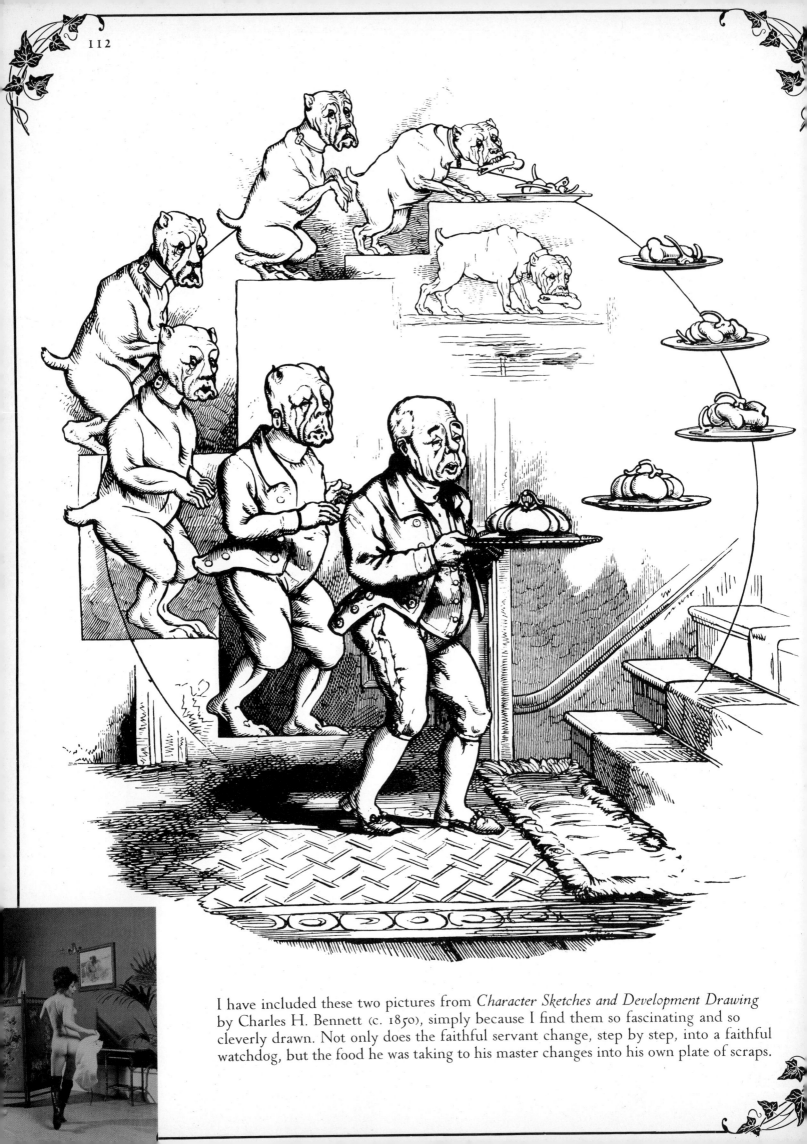

I have included these two pictures from *Character Sketches and Development Drawing* by Charles H. Bennett (c. 1850), simply because I find them so fascinating and so cleverly drawn. Not only does the faithful servant change, step by step, into a faithful watchdog, but the food he was taking to his master changes into his own plate of scraps.

Historical Section

Even more ingenious, this somewhat macabre portrait of a mugger of the time, consulting the turnip-watch of a previous victim, as he waits for his present prey to emerge from some Music Hall or supper-rooms. His origin is quickly traced to a muzzled and dangerous dancing-bear, while the watch becomes his padlock, and his cudgel the very post which holds him captive. This kind of meticulous and detailed drawing is, to me, one of the fascinations of Victorian illustrated humour—satirical or otherwise.

RINKO-MANIACAL RECOLLECTIONS

Pardon me but I believe
this is the tip of your nose.

The Pyramid

The Professional

CRUTCHES
ON
HIRE
EMBROCATION
&c

WAY OUT

After the battle

Somewhat later (about 1890) these very charming and funny drawings have a
distinctly saucy air—the girl hugging the curate in spite of herself, the pyramid of
bodies, male and female, piled up unceremoniously on the ice-rink; and the plump,
pretty, tearful maiden who is "horribly bruised, but she dare not rub herself in

RINKO-MANIACAL RECOLLECTIONS.

The Rink Boot

He hates rinking but he must bring himself down somehow

The impending cropper

I cannot mind my wheel Mother

Horribly bruised but she does not rule herself in public

Rink Dove

Taking a seat

Putting on "The hug"

A PERFECT MASTER OF HIS ART.

SOLDIER MODEL.

A COMING VICTIM.

FIELD MARSHALL K.C.

THE MAJOR.

THE DRUMMER.

public''. The coloured scraps, rescued from the discarded remains of late Victorian Christmas crackers, are tiny gems of caricature. But by now, of course, we have moved once again into the era of Grandaddie's sauce . . .

PROMOTER OF OTHERS CAPITAL AND INTEREST.

STOCK EXCHANGE.

CITY BUMBLE WITH HIS BAUBLE.

ALDERMAN MENU.

MY LORD.

MY LORD MAYOR KING OF COMMERCE.

MY LORD MAYOR'S JEAMES.

MODERN DICK WHITTINGTON.

Historical Section

... And "La Vie Parisienne" was already well ahead in that field:

(and here is a picture of the very field)

Historical Section

But as an end to the historical section, I have delved as far back as possible into history, and here present

THE FIRST JOKES EVER

A: Where are you going with that sack of horse manure?
B: I'm going to put it on my rhubarb.
A: That's funny—we usually have custard on ours.   (German, seventeenth century)

Man: Who is that in the mirror?
Jester (looks)*:* Why me, of course.
Man: Thank the Lord—I thought it was me!

(English, fifteenth century)

''Bottom Marks in History''
(Italian, sixteenth century)

Woman: This has been a wonderful broom. I've had it for twenty years, and it's only needed one new head and two handles.
(English, fifteenth century)

Appendix 2 Puzzles & Pastimes

A few of the many pictorial nonsenses indulged in, in days gone by:

Left—A puzzle in a cracker. Find the horse.
ANSWER—

BETWEEN THE LEGS OF THE MAN WHO IS PUSHING THE CAR

The two cut-outs are, I think, self-explanatory!

Below
To find out what the gentlemen are thinking, you must fold over the edge of the page ➡ until it meets the line drawn on the picture

PROMOTING.
PUZZLE, FIND THE HORSE.

TOM SMITH'S MOTOR CAR CRACKERS.

HOW DO THEY SEE YOU?

CUT OUT AND PLACE ON OWN NOSE

CUT OUT THESE CIRCLES

STICK FINGERS THROUGH AND WAGGLE

Germany

SCHILLER. MARIA STUART, FIESCO, WALLENSTEIN, JEANNE D'ARC

Un faune

L'Amore di Pierrot

View of the Pyrenees from the water. (See previous page)

Cut dotted lines and fold along edge of bath

Un beau Sauteur

Le Favorit

ON CLOSER INSPECTION

It will be found that these pictures (with the exception of the gruesome skull effect created by the one top centre) are, for the most part, made up of women.

Napoleon wrote to a contemporary, "The world appears to be made up of women"; and his own portrait (above, right) seems to go a long way towards proving him right.

Speaking of going a long way, the runners and riders here shown in the pictures on the left seem to be well capable of staying the distance, as they say, at Epsom.

Le Vainqueur

TRICKS OF THE EYE

Bring slowly towards the eye and watch effect.

Ma' honey

As you bring the picture nearer to your eyes, the dusky pair appear to kiss.

Bring slowly towards the eye and watch effect.

Drawing the stump.

Follow the instructions, and the dentist will appear to remove (and replace) the patient's molar.

Carry out the same actions, as above, and the lady will appear to be riding her bicycle with one leg over the handlebars.

PUZZLE PAGE
Study the pictures carefully

One of the girls appears in the same pose twice. Now answer the following questions:
A. Is it the second girl from the right at the bottom, or not? B. What does it matter?

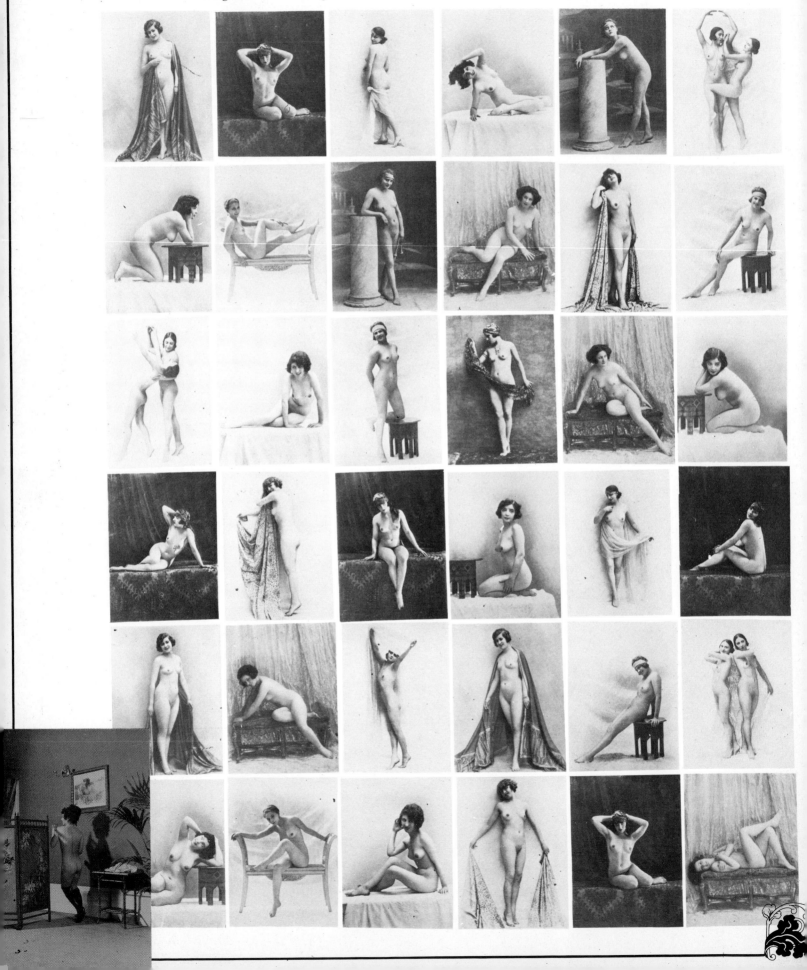

Appendix 3
Bump-reading for pleasure and profit

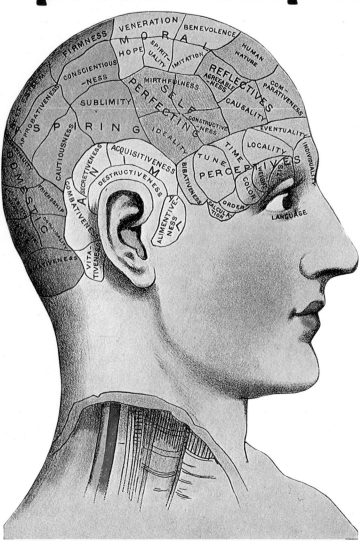

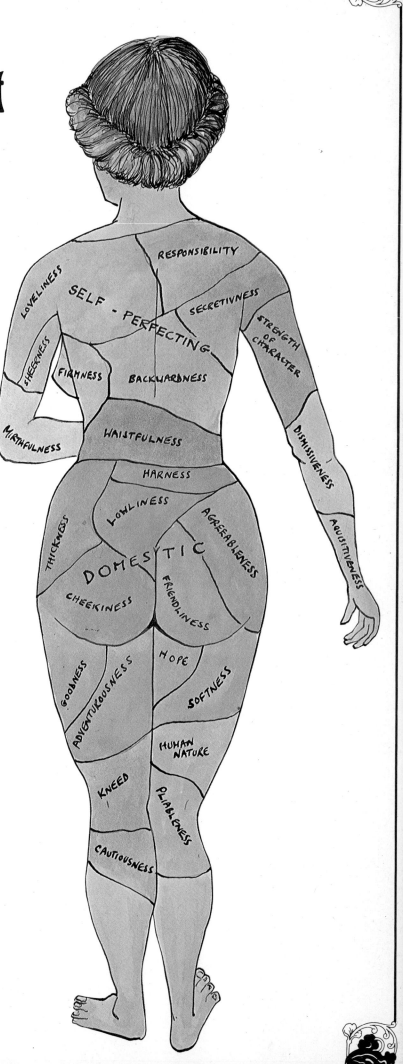

In man, it is called Phrenology. But, as Voltaire was once heard to remark, "A woman's brains are not in her head alone, but all over her body."

This chart is therefore offered for amateur phrenologists everywhere, in the hope that it will be of assistance in the interpretation of bump-reading in women.

Female Bump-reader at work

Answers to Correspondents

Fig.5.
Correct position
of the body
in writing.

Fig.6.
Deformity
of the spine
caused by
incorrect position
in writing.

1. *To Mr. F. W. D. of Oxford:*
I have pleasure in re-printing the picture you request, and trust that you will always adopt this position when writing to me in future—Ed.

P.S. It is not necessary to wear the sailor-suit, if inconvenient.

2. *To Miss Janet T. of Chester:*
The person who holds the record for losing weight is Mr. Arthur Godbolt, of Huddersfield, who lost seventeen stone in twenty-nine days. His picture is shown on the right.

3. *To W. M. of Highgate:*
If you are so well-known that it is impossible for you to go into the street without being recognised, why not adopt the disguise of a camera man, as shown? With your head under the cloth, you can wander around the park, enter restaurants, attend balls, etc., confident that passers-by will not give you a second glance.

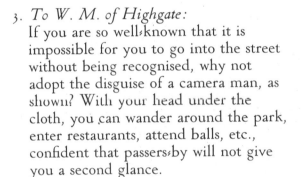

4. *To Miss Muriel B., the Rosycheeks Nudist Camp, Chorley Wood:*
Your most interesting picture of yourself and your friend observing the goings-on behind the bush, did, I must admit, stump your Editor for a while; but I am now quite certain that it is, in fact, another of your friends engaged in fitting a new sheet of paper into her typewriter. Am I correct? (My first surmise I discarded almost at once, bearing in mind the large number of stinging nettles in your area.)

MISS EDNA MAY

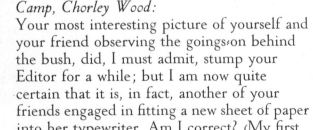

5. *To Mrs. B. D., of Wimbledon:*
The above is an example of juxtaposition. What your husband says is quite wrong.

This lady is, of course, astride a somewhat higher-class bottle than the one which adorns the front of this book; the gap is widened more than somewhat when one realises that, as this etching was published round about 1890, the champagne just about to bubble forth from this particular magnum must be of a vintage which today would be priceless.

And so indeed, in my opinion, is the picture; and the lady provides for us a fitting end to what I hope you will consider to have been a generous helping of SAUCE

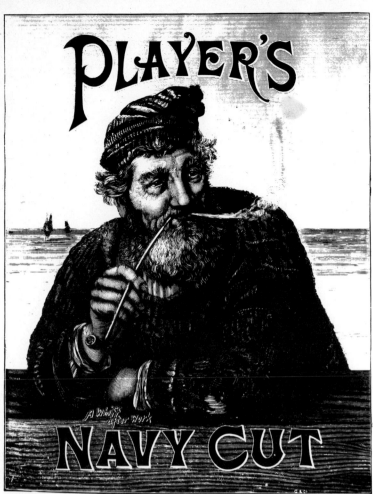

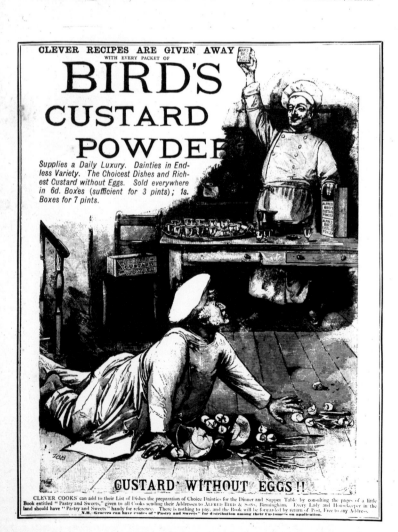

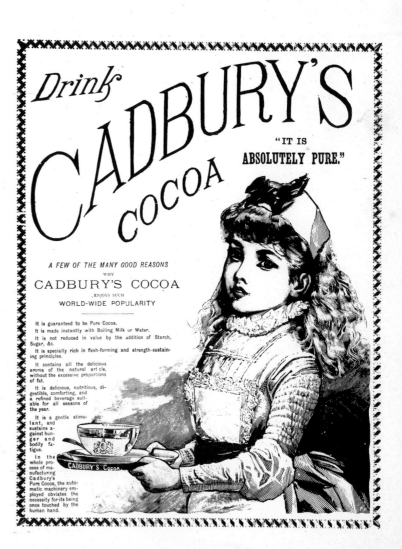